Numbers Tracing Math Practice Workbook
Preschool & Kindergarten:

Number Tracing book (1-100) for Preschoolers & Kindergarteners

P9-EEI-157

This book belongs to:

_____

This is a number writing book that helps kids learn to write numbers and number words in a fun and engaging way.

It is organized in a progressively skill building way for kids to develop confidence to write numbers.

This book requires guidance from a teacher, parent or care giver to help the child practice number writing.

You can photocopy parts of this book for use with a family member.

Teachers are welcome to reproduce some worksheets from this book for their class only. However, teachers are not allowed to reproduce worksheets for other teachers or for entire school use. Please encourage other teachers to buy their own copy of this book!

Meet Jojo.
Jojo is a curious elephant.
He loves to learn and play.
Learn to write numbers along with Jojo!

This Number Tracing workbook is divided into the following parts:

Part 1: Number Practice:

Trace numbers (0-20) and practice writing them on your own

Show the numbers with the help of your fingers

Part 2: Learning Number Words:

Revise the letters of the alphabet

Trace the number words and say them out loud as you write

Part 3: Activities, Counting and Simple Addition:

Play number game activities

Count and color the objects

Add two numbers by counting the stars

Part 4: Writing Numbers from 21-100

Trace the numbers and practice writing them on your own

Practice writing numbers from 1 - 100

Kids can use a pencil, light color marker or highlighter
to trace the dotted numbers and number words.
Use color pencils to color the objects.

1 2 3 4 5 6 7 8 9 10

11 12 13 14 15 16 17 18 19 20

Hi!

My name is Sujatha Lalgudi. I sincerely hope you find my number tracing book to be helpful and fun.

Write to me at **sujatha.lalgudi@gmail.com** with the subject:

Number Trace along with **your kid's name** to receive:

- Additional practice worksheets.
- A name tracing worksheet so your kid can practice writing their own name.
- An Award Certificate in Color to gift your child!

If you liked this book, please leave me a review on Amazon! Your kind reviews and comments will encourage me to make more books like this.

Thank you
Sujatha Lalgudi

Part 1:

Number Practice

Show numbers with the help of your fingers.
Trace and practice the numbers.
Try writing them on your own on the blank line.

You are AMAZING!

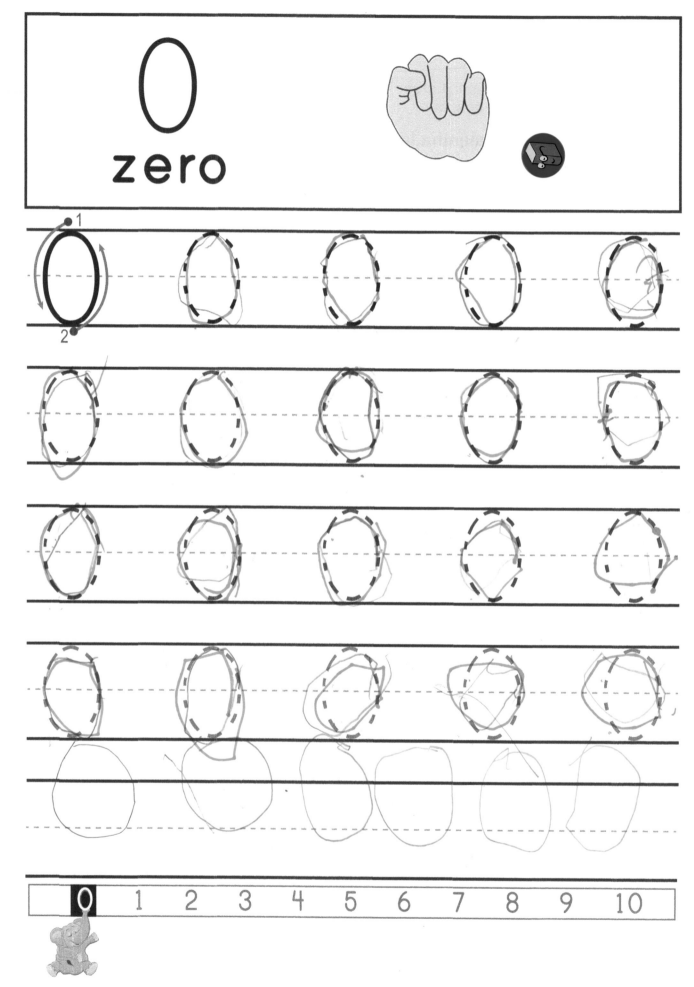

0 zero

0 1 2 3 4 5 6 7 8 9 10

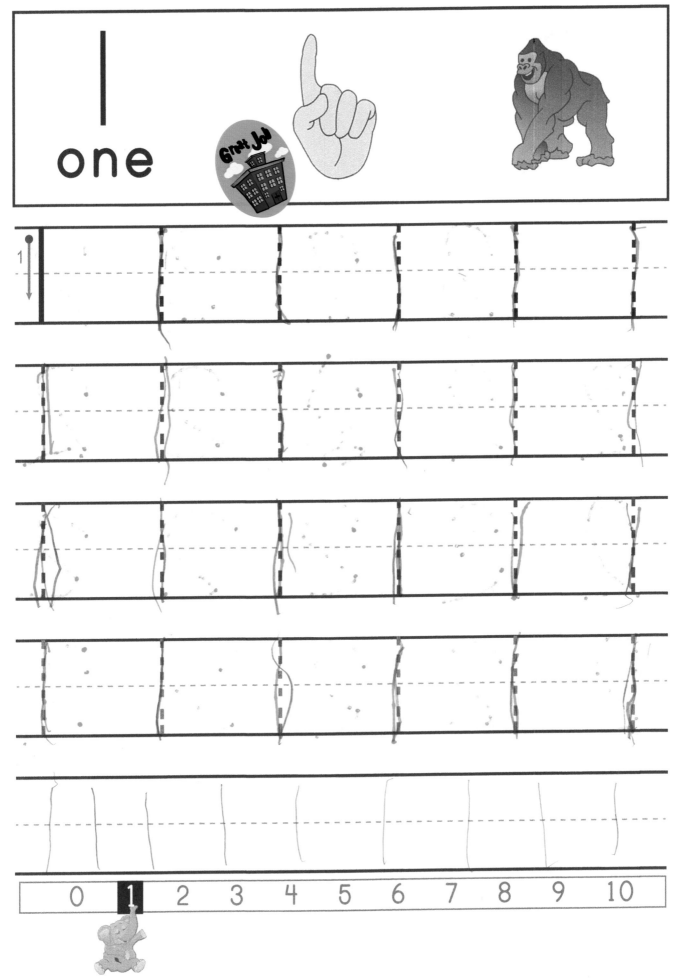

one

0 **1** 2 3 4 5 6 7 8 9 10

2
two

2

2 2 2 2 2

2 2 2 2 2

2 2 2 2 2

2 2 2 2 2

2 2 2 2 2 2

| 0 | 1 | **2** | 3 | 4 | 5 | 6 | 7 | 8 | 9 | 10 |

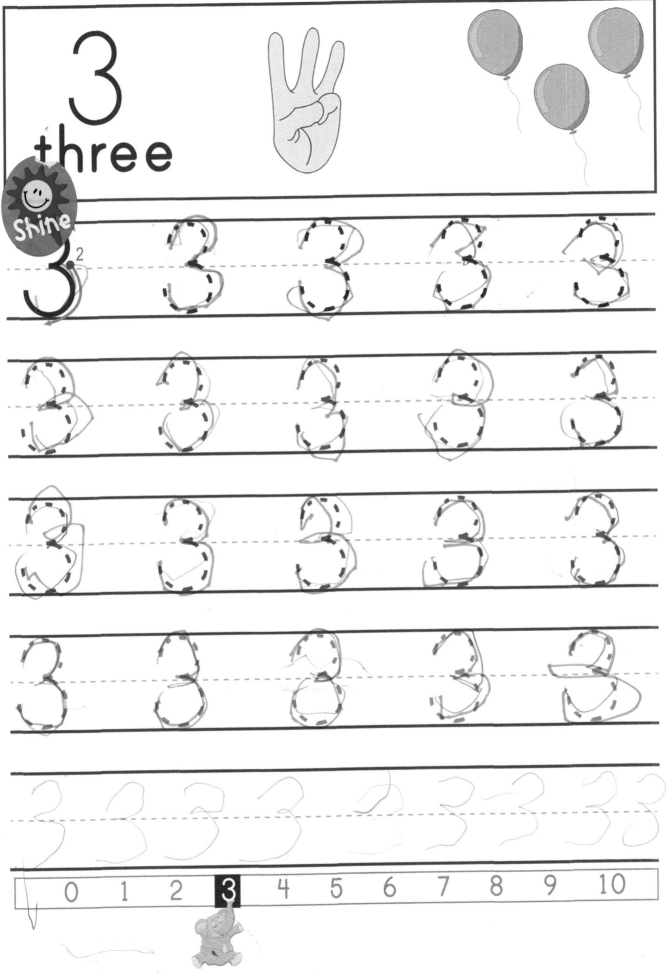

3
three

0 1 2 **3** 4 5 6 7 8 9 10

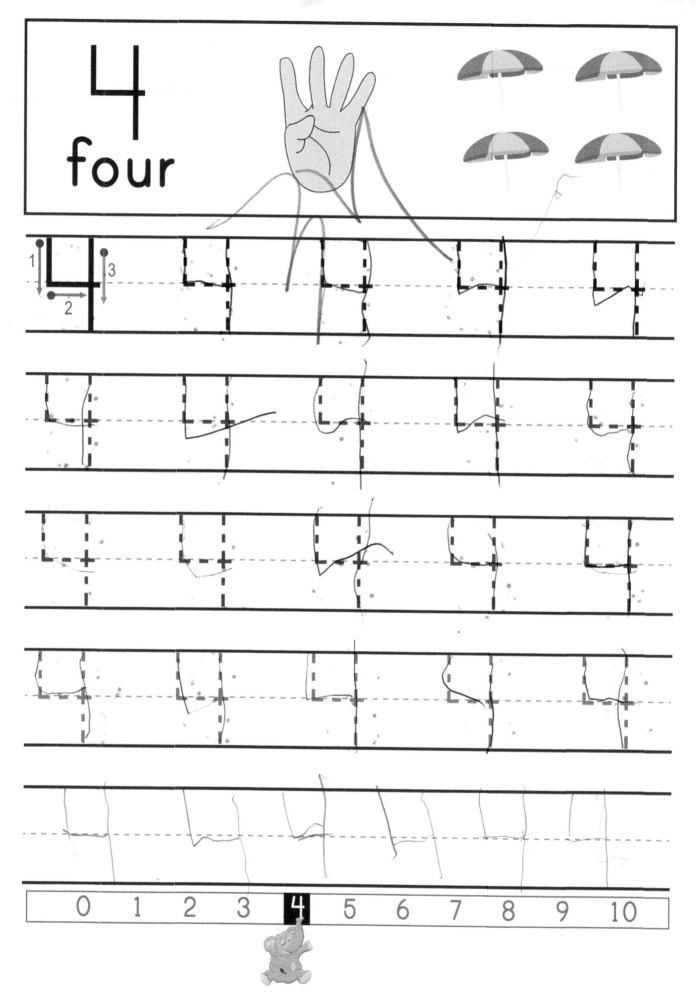

4
four

| 0 | 1 | 2 | 3 | **4** | 5 | 6 | 7 | 8 | 9 | 10 |

5
five

WAY to GO!

0 1 2 3 4 **5** 6 7 8 9 10

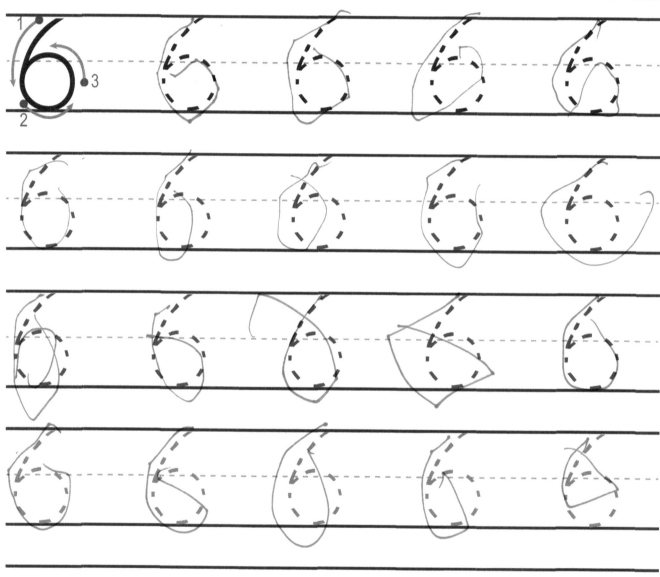

| 0 | 1 | 2 | 3 | 4 | 5 | 6 | 7 | 8 | 9 | 10 |

7
seven

0 1 2 3 4 5 6 **7** 8 9 10

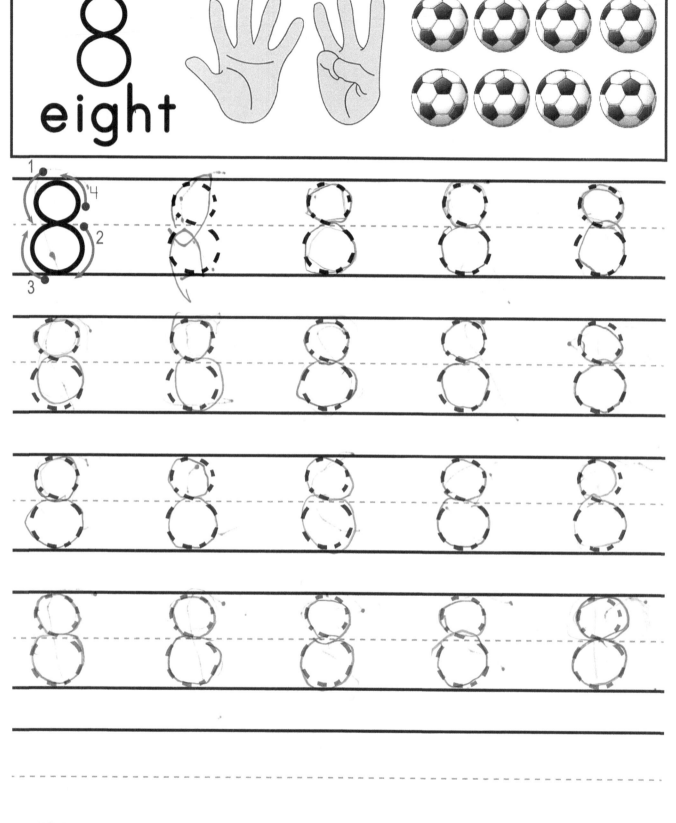

8
eight

0 1 2 3 4 5 6 7 **8** 9 10

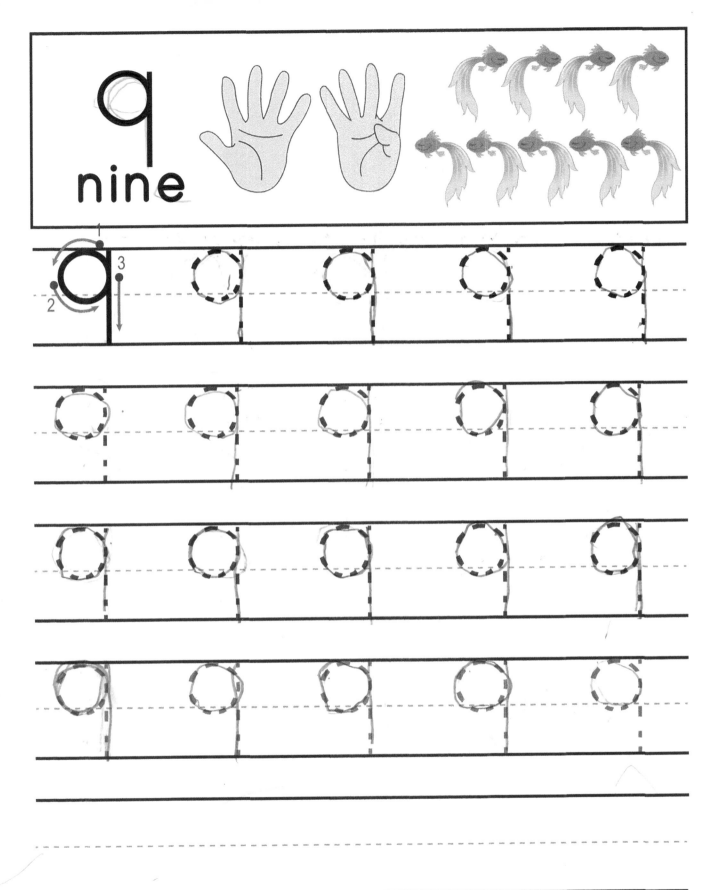

9 nine

0 1 2 3 4 5 6 7 8 9 10

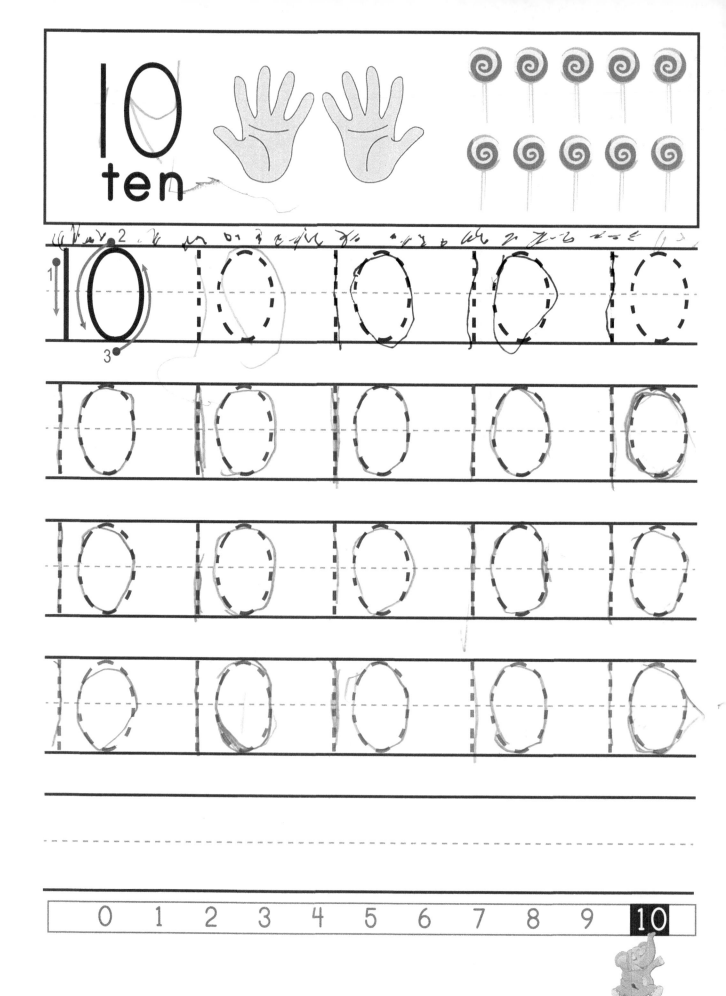

10
ten

0 1 2 3 4 5 6 7 8 9 10

11 eleven

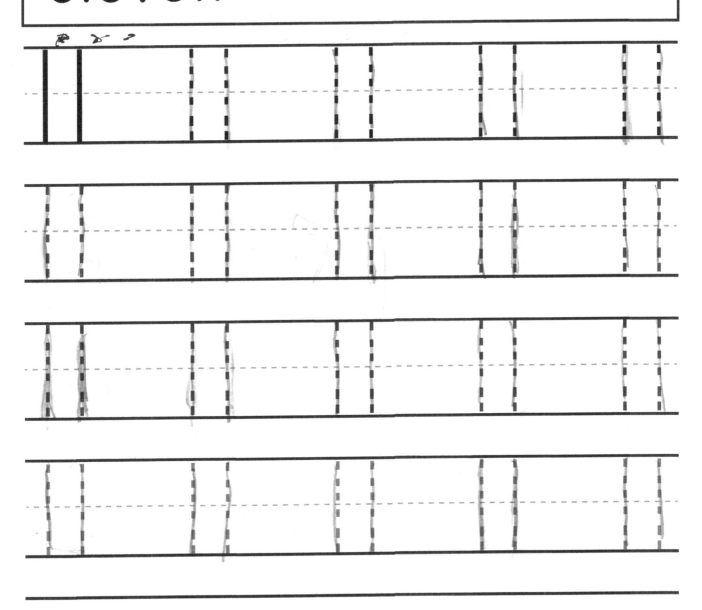

12
twelve

12 12 12 12

12 12 12 12

12 12 12 12

12 12 12 12

13
thirteen

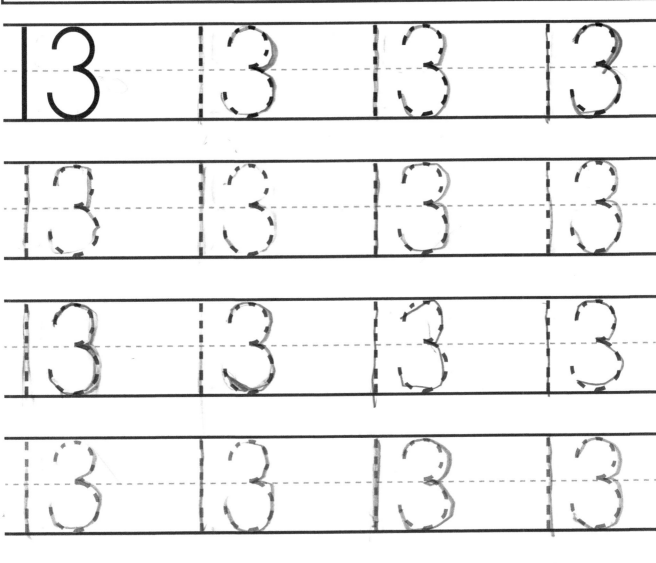

13 13 13 13

13 13 13 13

13 13 13 13

13 13 13 13

| 11 | 12 | **13** | 14 | 15 | 16 | 17 | 18 | 19 | 20 |

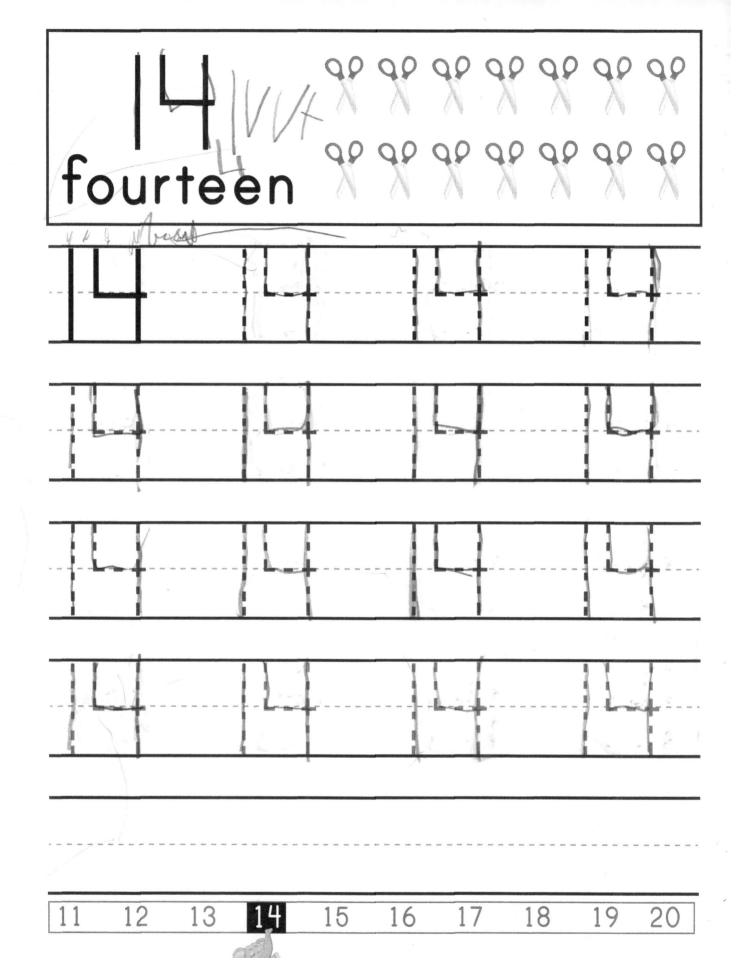

14
fourteen

15
fifteen

15   15   15   15

15   15   15   15

15   15   15   15

15   15   15   15

| 11 | 12 | 13 | 14 | 15 | 16 | 17 | 18 | 19 | 20 |

16
sixteen

16 6 6 6

6 6 6 6

6 6 6 6

6 6 6 6

| 11 | 12 | 13 | 14 | 15 | 16 | 17 | 18 | 19 | 20 |

17
seventeen

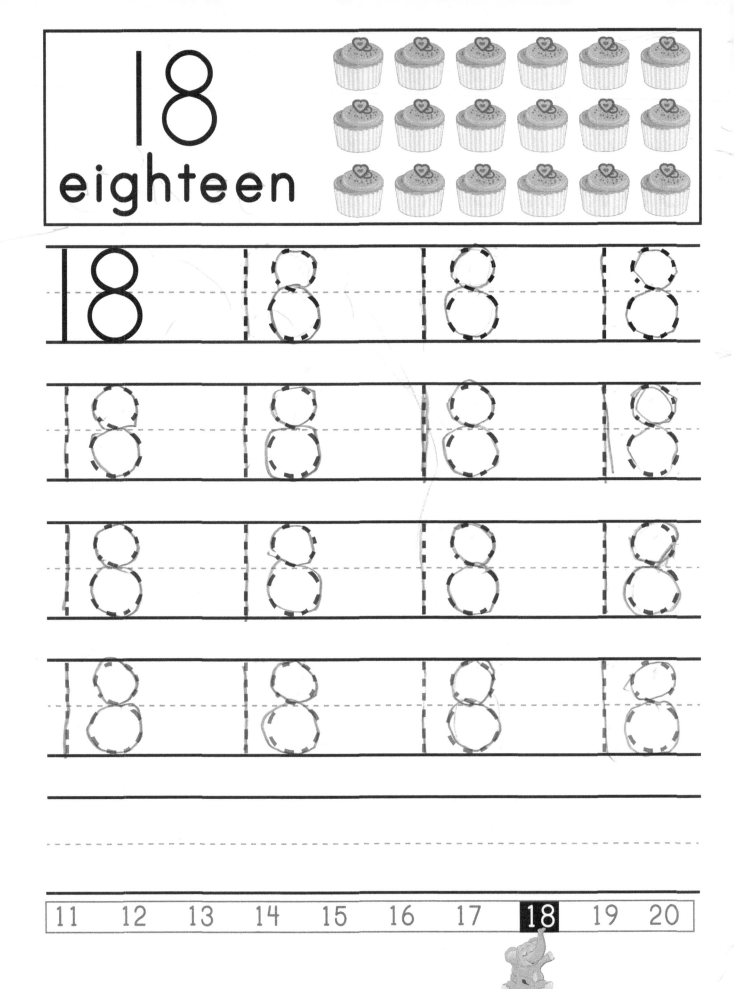

18
eighteen

11 12 13 14 15 16 17 **18** 19 20

22

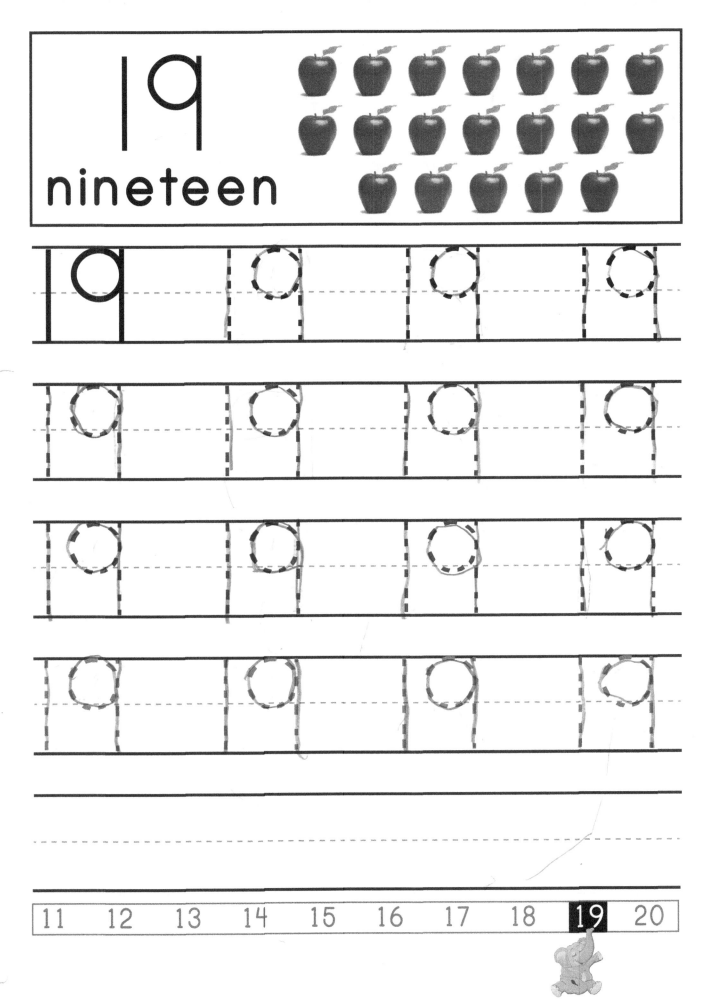

19
nineteen

20
twenty

| 11 | 12 | 13 | 14 | 15 | 16 | 17 | 18 | 19 | 20 |

Part 2:

Learning Number Words

Practice tracing the letters of the alphabet.
Trace the number words and
read them out loud.

You are
brilliant!

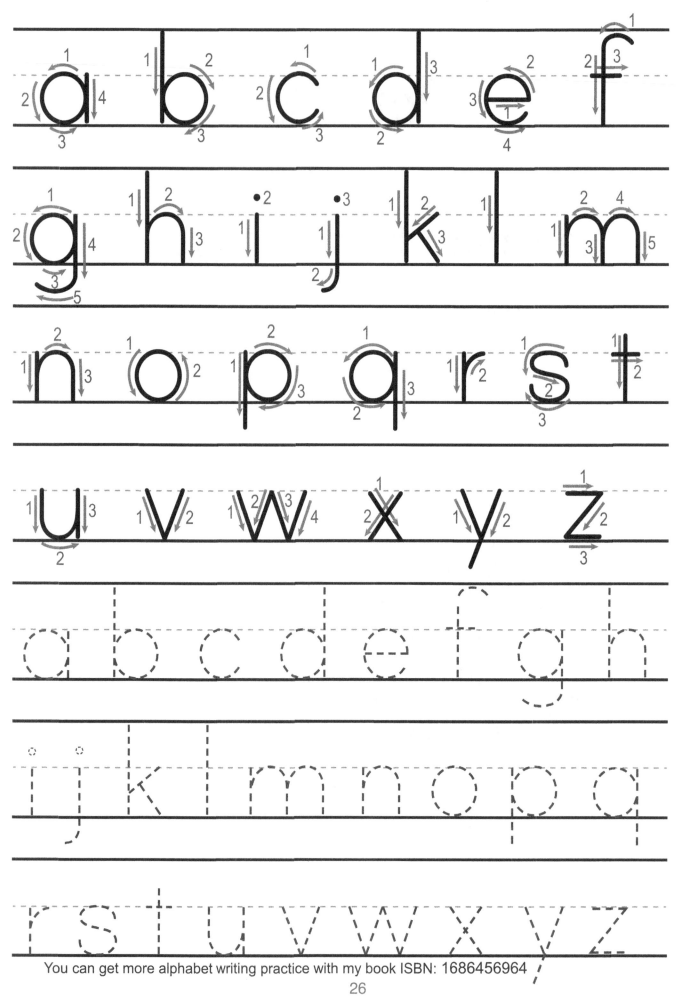

0   zero

zero   zero

zero   zero

zero   zero

zero   zero

zero   zero

| **0** | 1 | 2 | 3 | 4 | 5 | 6 | 7 | 8 | 9 | 10 |

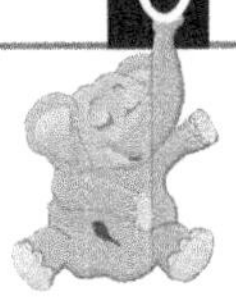

one one one

one one one

one one one

one one one

one one one

| 0 | 1 | 2 | 3 | 4 | 5 | 6 | 7 | 8 | 9 | 10 |

two two two

two two two

two wo two

two two two

two two two

| 0 | 1 | **2** | 3 | 4 | 5 | 6 | 7 | 8 | 9 | 10 |

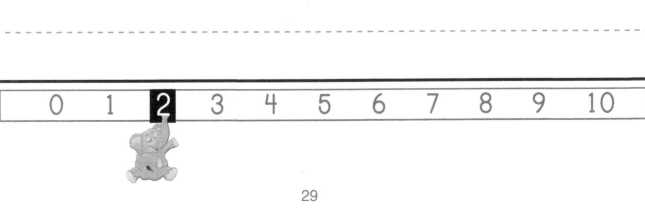

3 three ☆☆☆

three three

three three

three three

three three

three three

| 0 | 1 | 2 | **3** | 4 | 5 | 6 | 7 | 8 | 9 | 10 |

4 four ☆☆☆☆

four four

four four

four four

four four

four four

5 five ☆☆☆☆☆

| 0 | 1 | 2 | 3 | 4 | **5** | 6 | 7 | 8 | 9 | 10 |

6 six ☆☆☆☆☆☆

six six six

six six six

six six six

six six six

six six six

0	1	2	3	4	5	**6**	7	8	9	10

seven seven

seven seven

seven seven

seven seven

seven seven

| 0 | 1 | 2 | 3 | 4 | 5 | 6 | 7 | 8 | 9 | 10 |

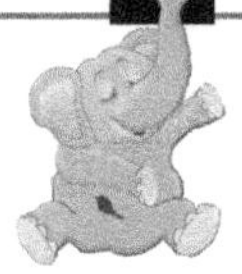

8 eight ☆☆☆☆☆☆☆☆

0	1	2	3	4	5	6	7	8	9	10

9 nine ☆☆☆☆☆☆☆☆

nine   nine

nine   nine

nine   nine

nine   nine

nine   nine

| 0 | 1 | 2 | 3 | 4 | 5 | 6 | 7 | 8 | **9** | 10 |

10	ten	☆☆☆☆☆☆☆☆☆☆

ten ten ten

ten ten ten

ten ten ten

ten ten ten

ten ten ten

| 0 | 1 | 2 | 3 | 4 | 5 | 6 | 7 | 8 | 9 | 10 |

11 eleven ☆☆☆☆☆☆☆☆☆☆☆

eleven

eleven

eleven

eleven

eleven

11	12	13	14	15	16	17	18	19	20

12 twelve ☆☆☆☆☆☆☆☆☆☆☆☆

twelve

twelve

twelve

twelve

twelve

13 thirteen ☆★★★★★★★★★★★☆

thirteen

thirteen

thirteen

thirteen

| 11 | 12 | **13** | 14 | 15 | 16 | 17 | 18 | 19 | 20 |

14 fourteen

⭐⭐⭐⭐⭐⭐⭐
⭐⭐⭐⭐⭐⭐⭐

fourteen

fourteen

fourteen

fourteen

fourteen

| 11 | 12 | 13 | **14** | 15 | 16 | 17 | 18 | 19 | 20 |

15 fifteen

fifteen

fifteen

fifteen

fifteen

fifteen

| 11 | 12 | 13 | 14 | **15** | 16 | 17 | 18 | 19 | 20 |

16 sixteen

sixteen

sixteen

sixteen

sixteen

sixteen

17 seventeen

seventeen

seventeen

seventeen

seventeen

seventeen

| 11 | 12 | 13 | 14 | 15 | 16 | **17** | 18 | 19 | 20 |

44

18 eighteen

eighteen

eighteen

eighteen

eighteen

eighteen

| 11 | 12 | 13 | 14 | 15 | 16 | 17 | **18** | 19 | 20 |

19 nineteen

nineteen

nineteen

nineteen

nineteen

nineteen

| 11 | 12 | 13 | 14 | 15 | 16 | 17 | 18 | 19 | 20 |

20 twenty

twenty

twenty

twenty

twenty

twenty

Part 3:

Activities
Play the number game activities.

Counting
Count the objects and color them.
Show the number you counted
with your fingers.
*Use the picture of the hand as a reference.
Write the number you counted.

Simple Addition
Add the numbers.
Use the stars to count the total.
Write down the answer.

COLOR BY NUMBER
Color the Mandala using the Color Chart

1 - Red 2 - Orange 3 - Light Blue
4 - Dark Blue 5 - Light Green 6 - Dark Green 7 - Brown
8 - Yellow 9 - Violet 10 - Pink

CONNECT THE DOTS

Draw the Kangaroo's tail by
connecting the numbered dots from 1-20

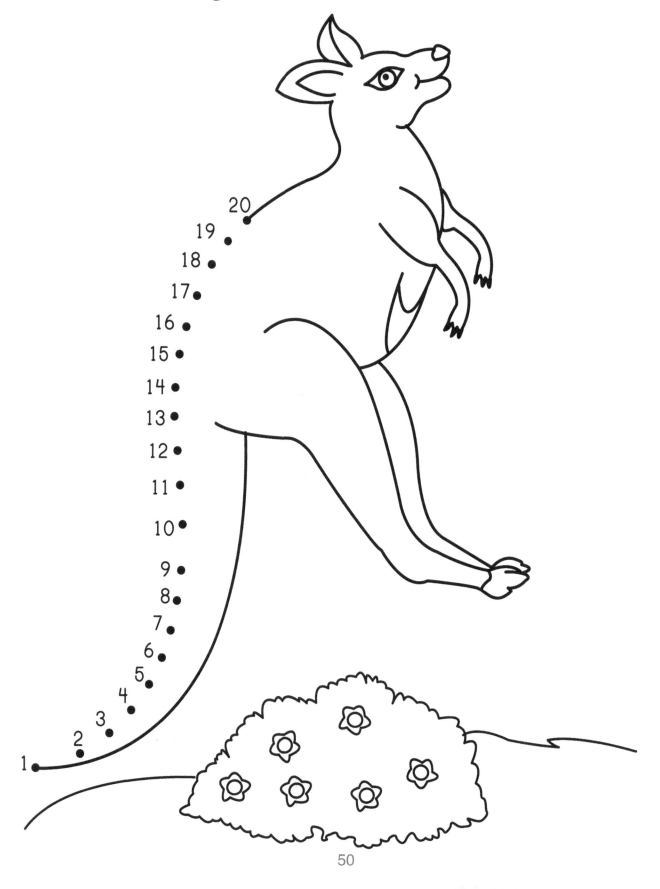

Counting

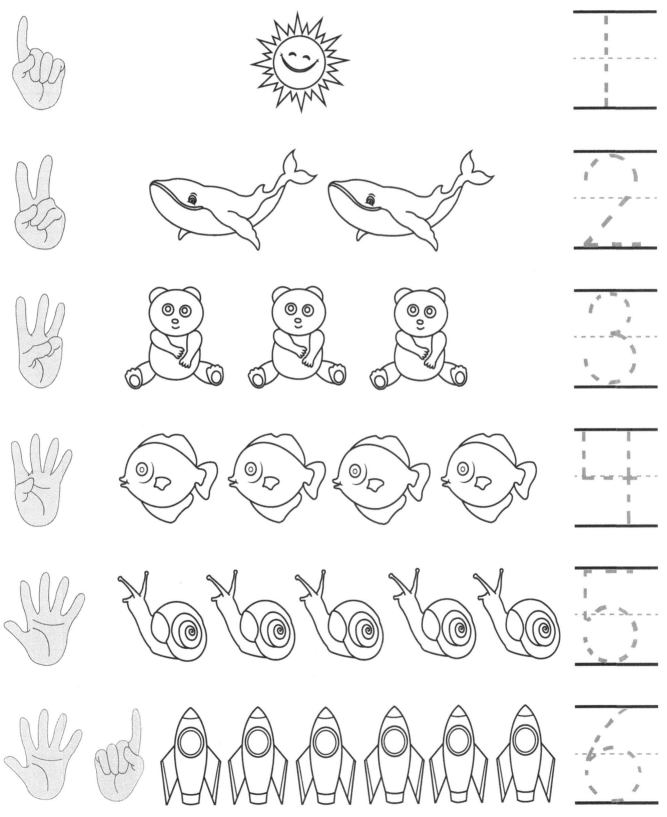

Counting

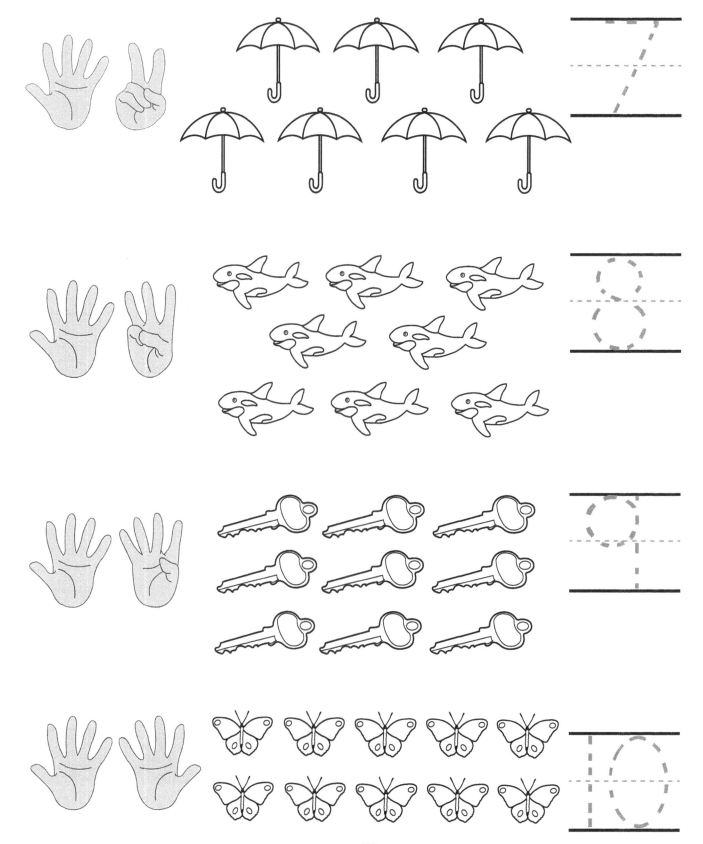

Counting Dice

1 = 🌼 1

2 = 🌼🌼 2

3 = 🌼🌼🌼 3

4 = 🌼🌼🌼🌼 4

5 = 🌼🌼🌼🌼🌼 5

6 = 🌼🌼🌼🌼🌼🌼 6

Simple Addition

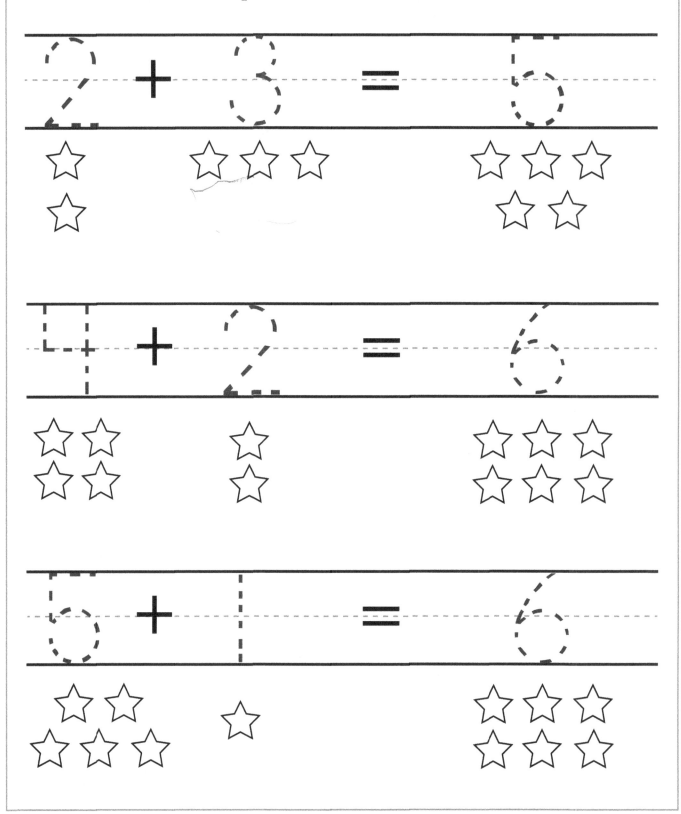

Simple Addition

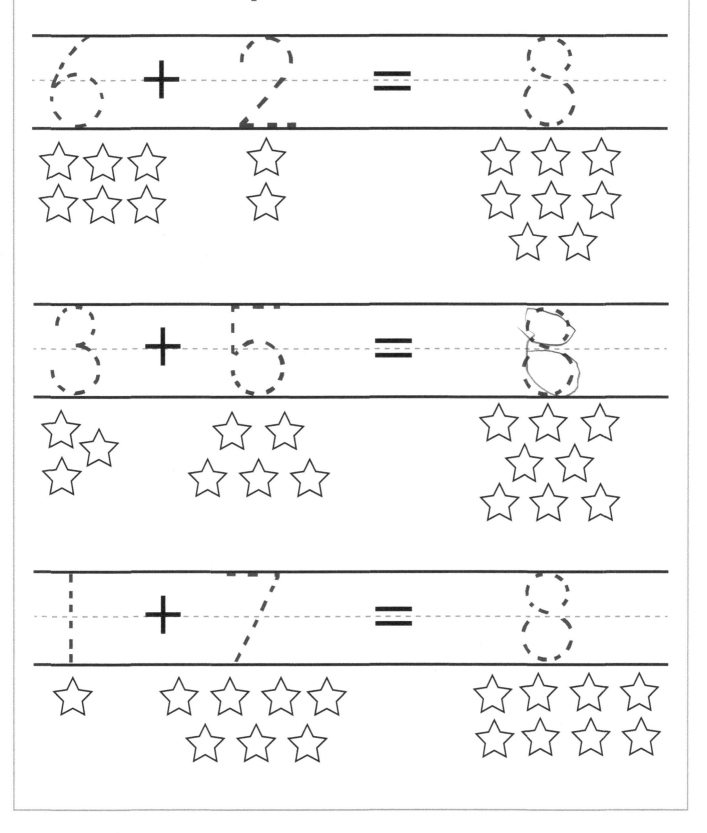

Simple Addition

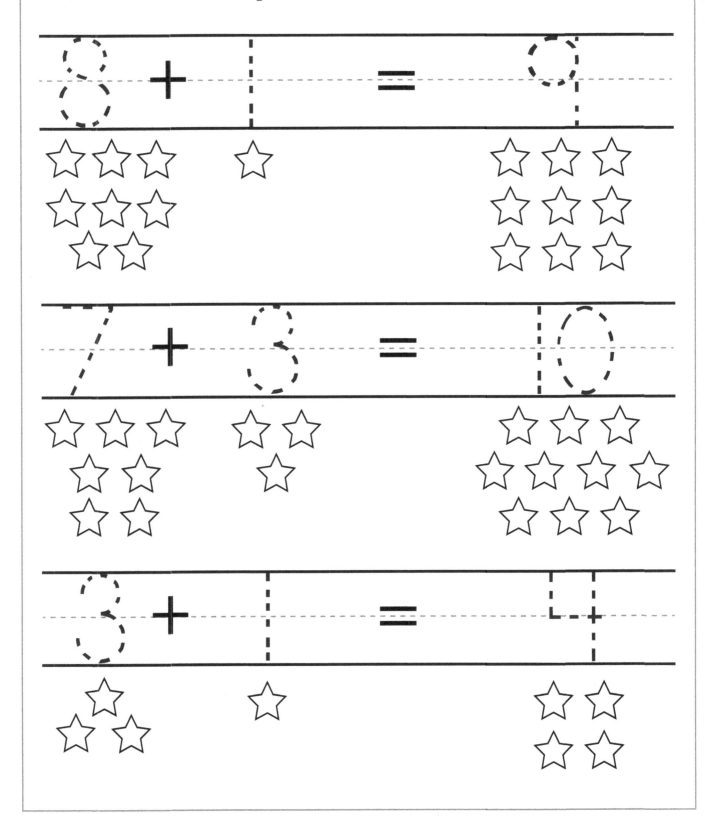

Simple Addition

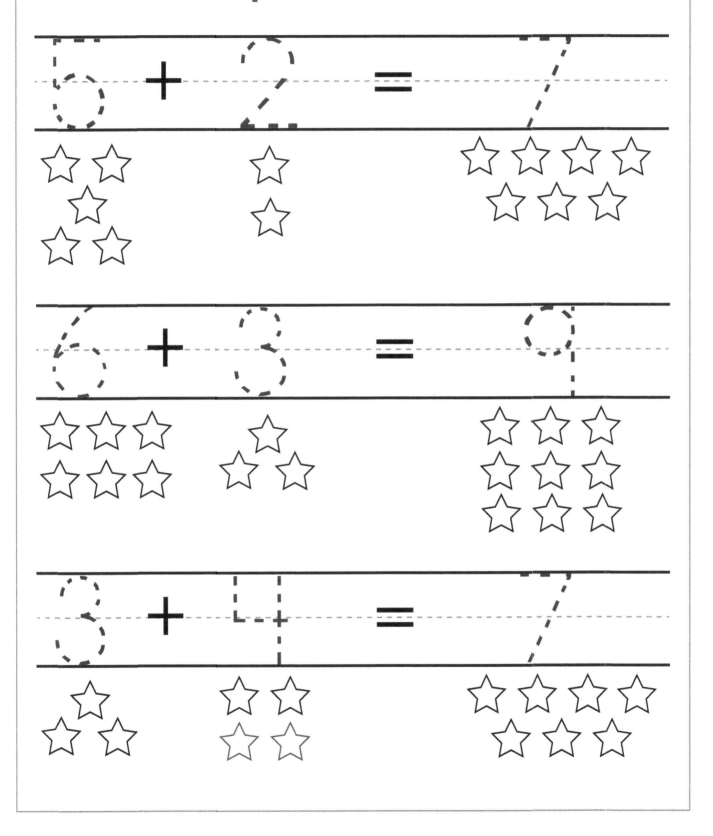

Simple Addition

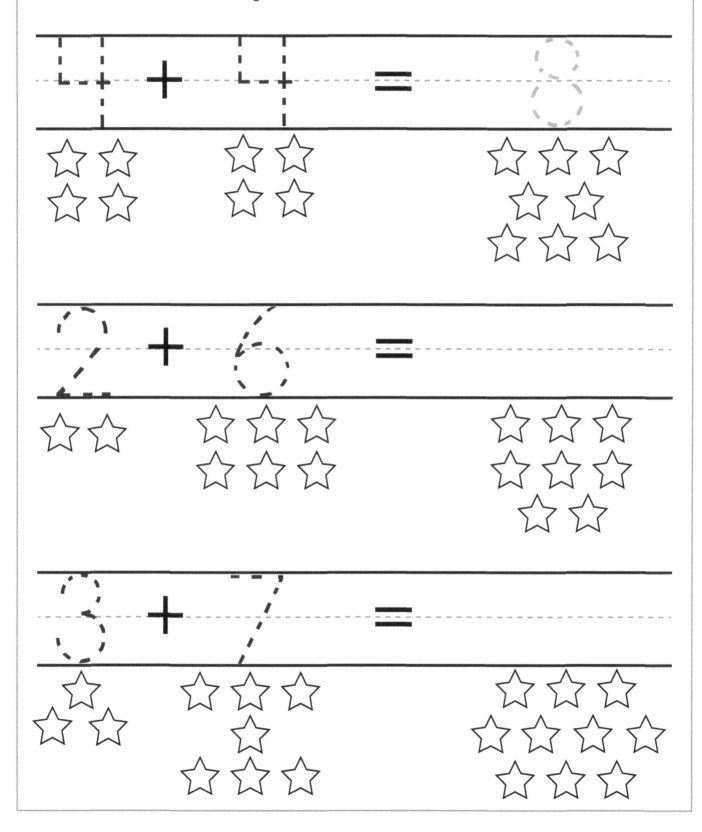

Simple Addition

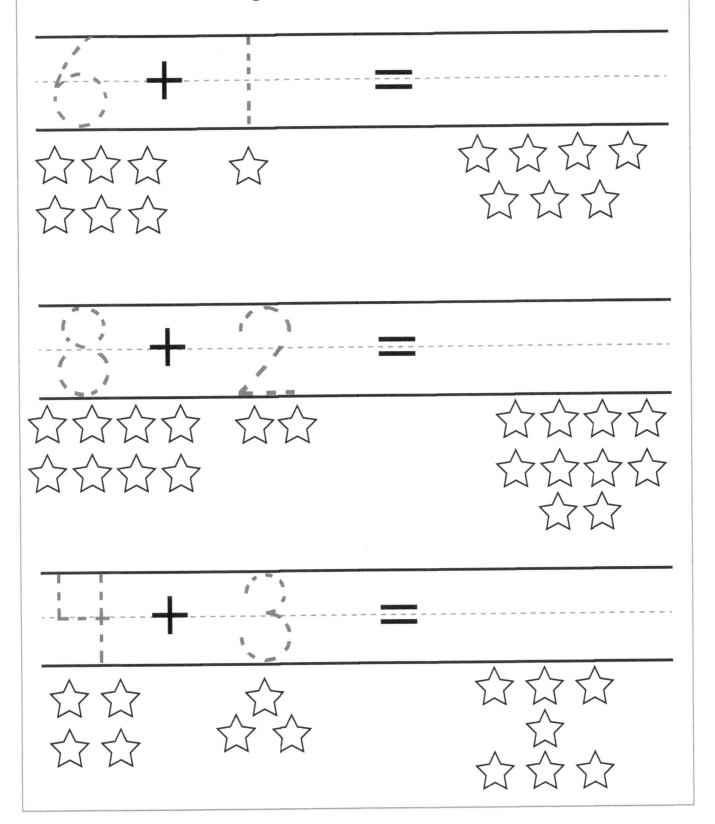

Simple Addition

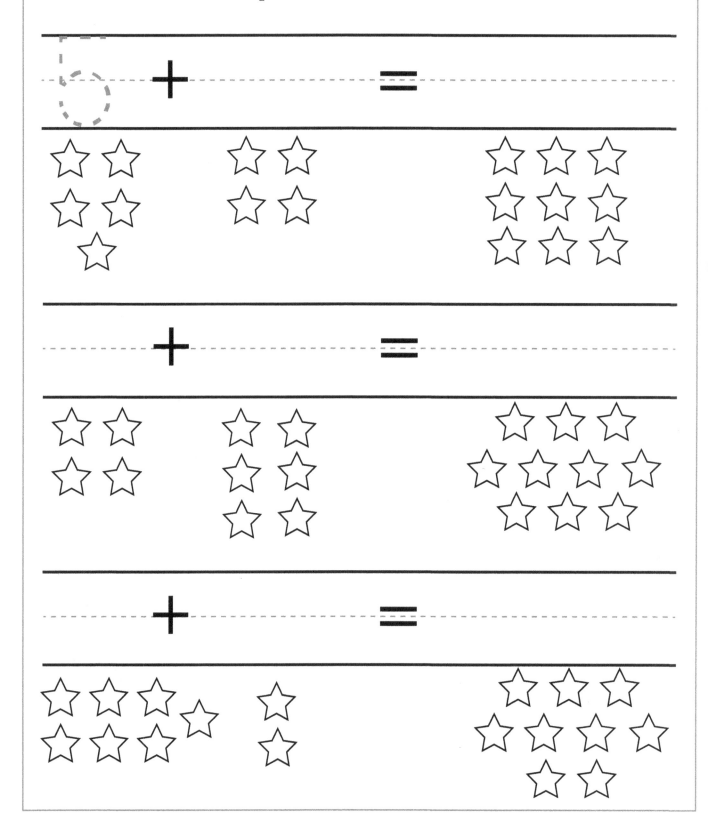

Simple Addition

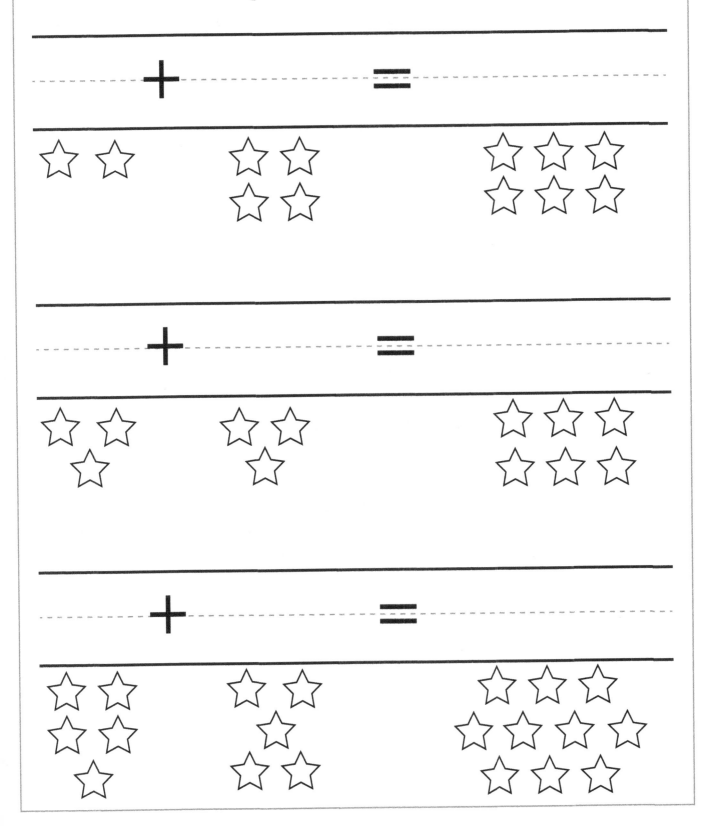

Part 7:

Write Numbers from 21-100

You will now be writing the numbers
in a smaller size.
Trace each number and say the number out loud.
Practice writing the number on your own
in the blank space.
Use your best handwriting!

You are
good at this!

21   twenty-one

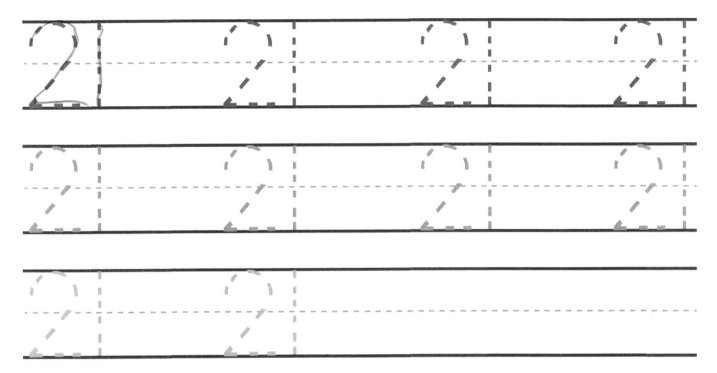

22   twenty-two

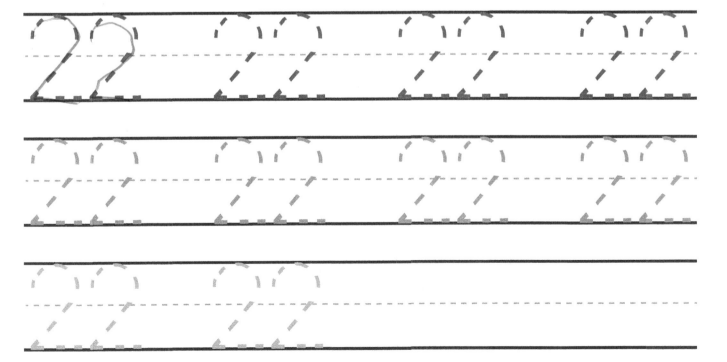

23   twenty-three

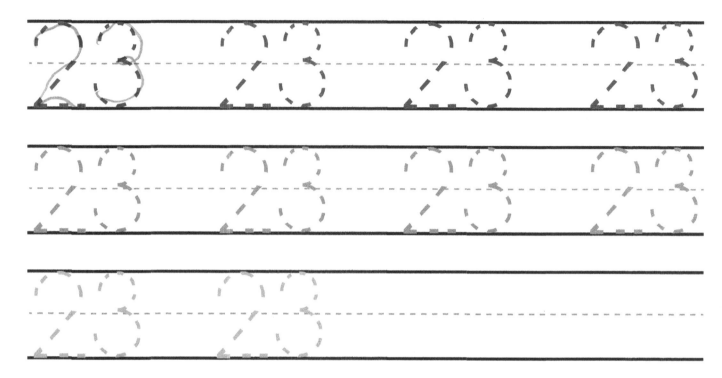

24   twenty-four

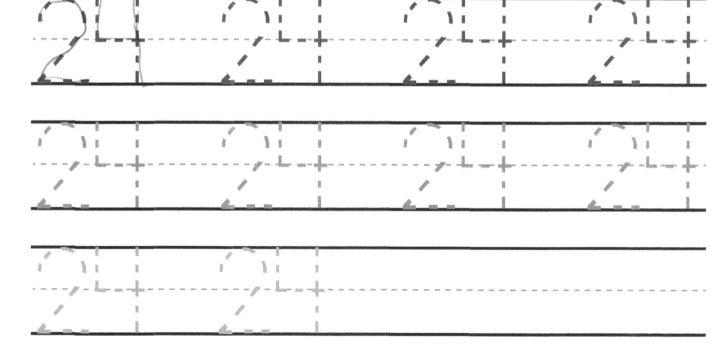

25 twenty-five

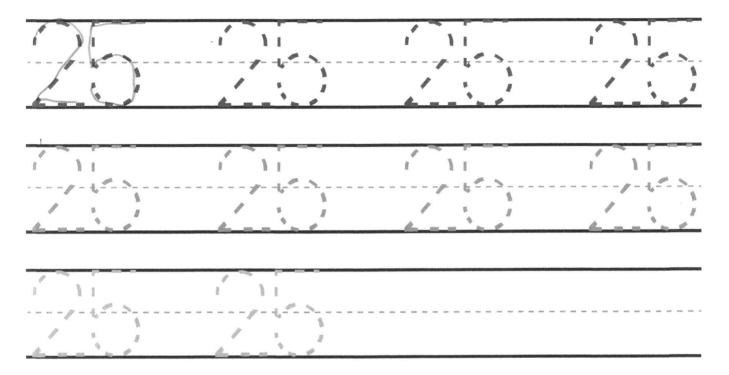

26 twenty-six

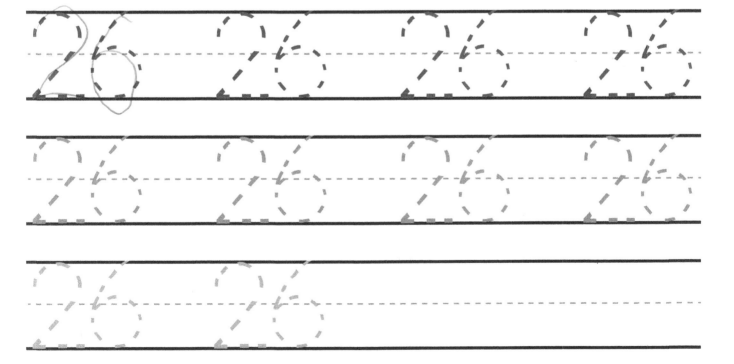

27 twenty-seven

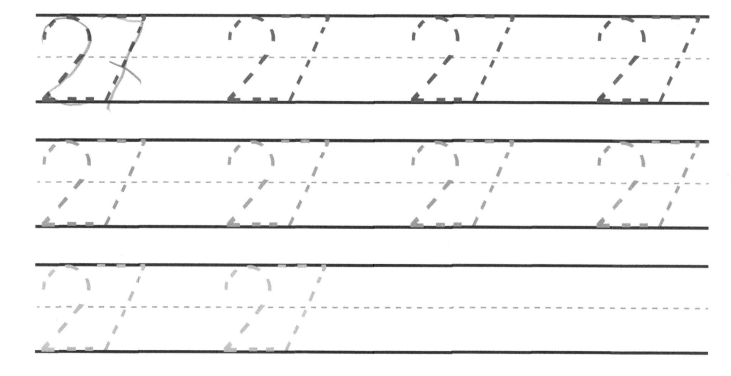

28 twenty-eight

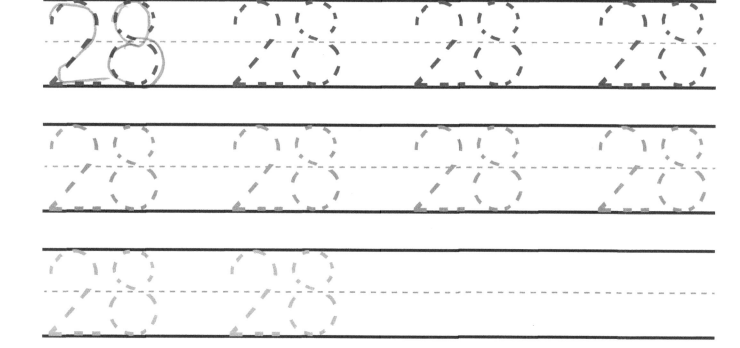

29 twenty-nine

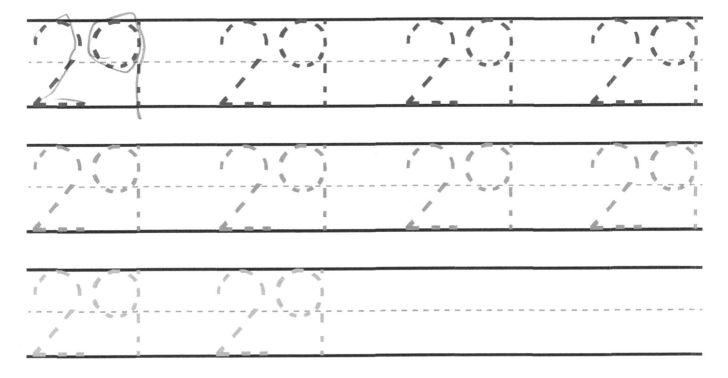

30 thirty

31 thirty-one

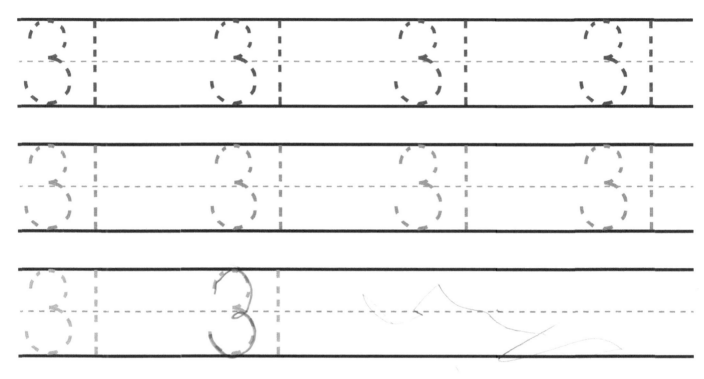

32 thirty-two

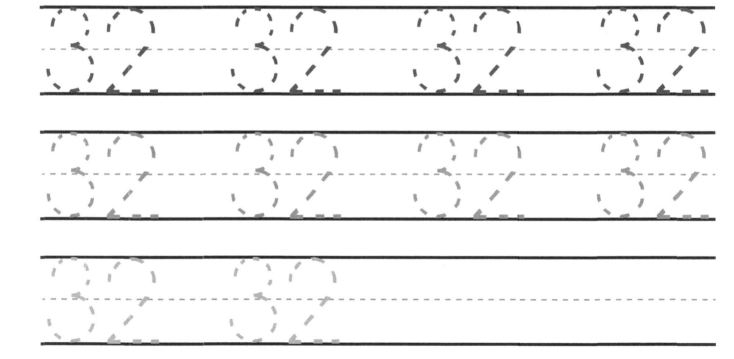

33 thirty-three

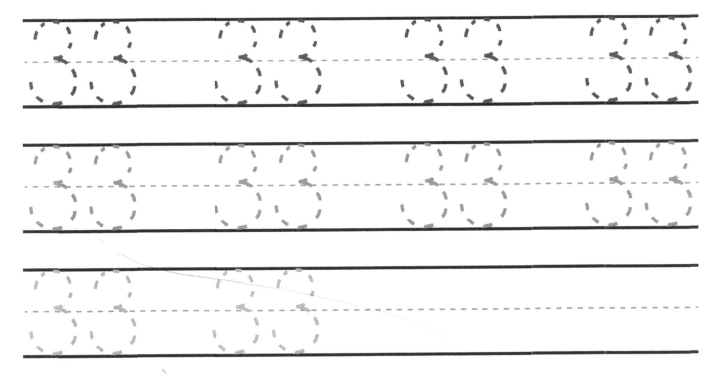

34 thirty-four

35 thirty-five

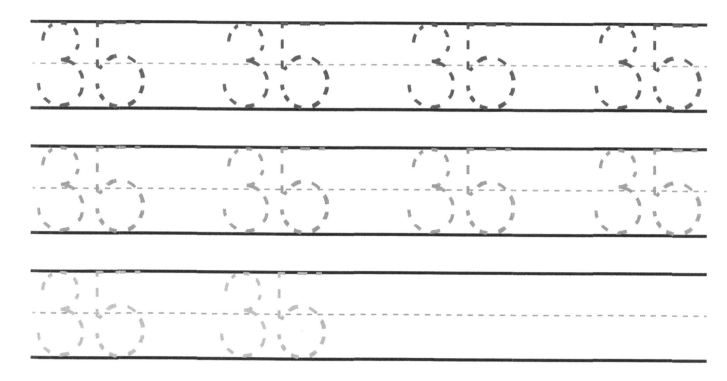

36 thirty-six

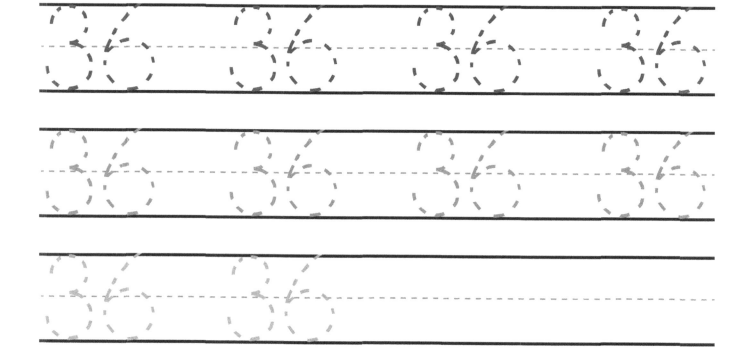

37 thirty-seven

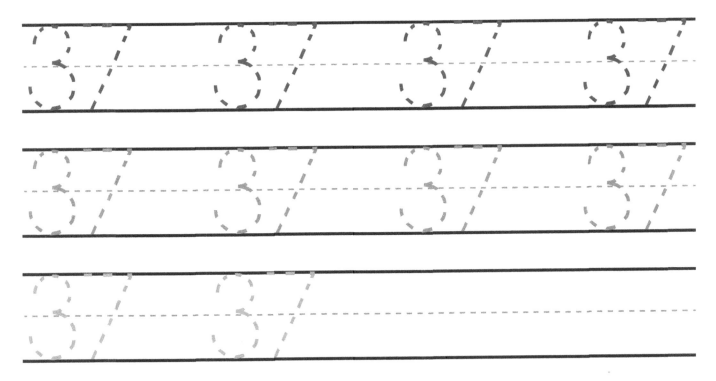

38 thirty-eight

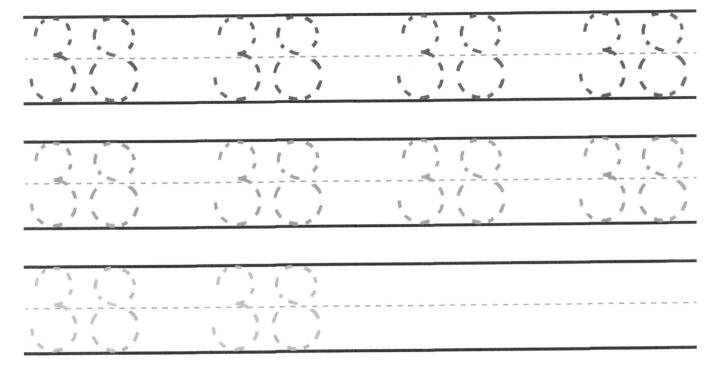

39 thirty-nine

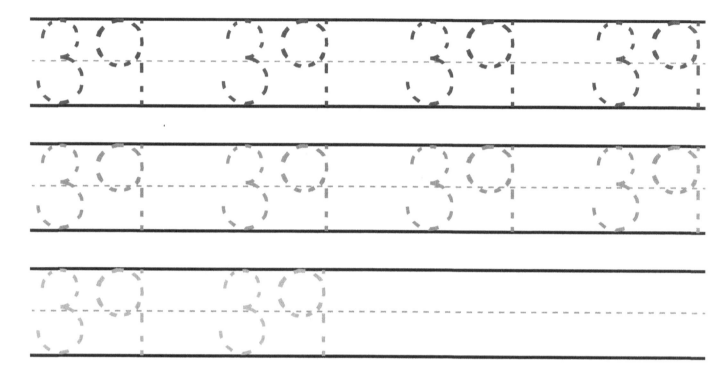

40 forty

41 forty-one

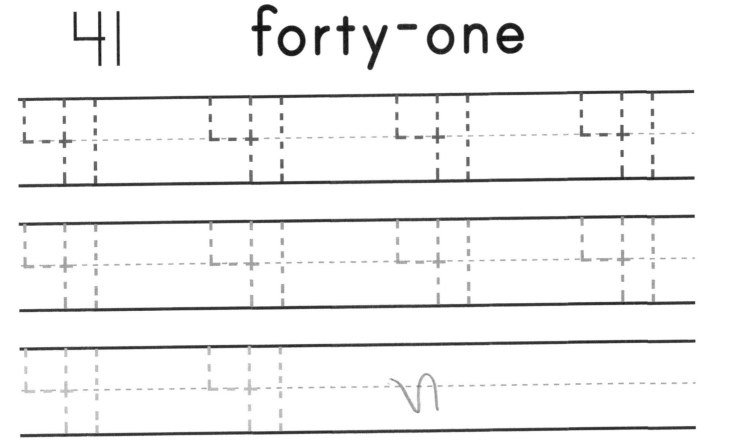

42 forty-two

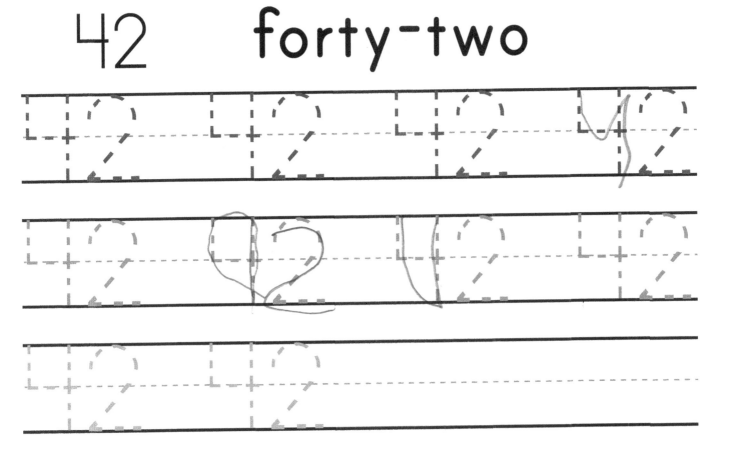

43 forty-three

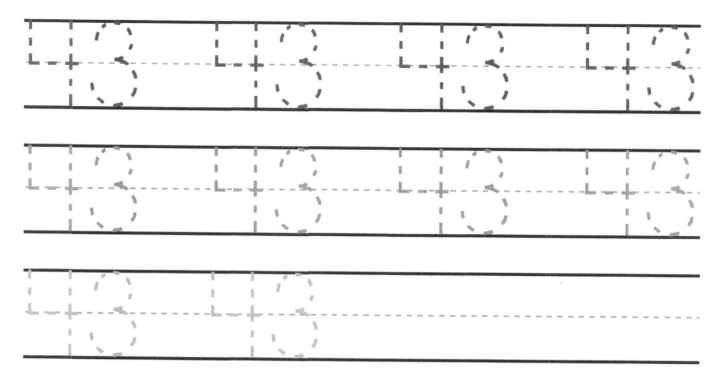

44 forty-four

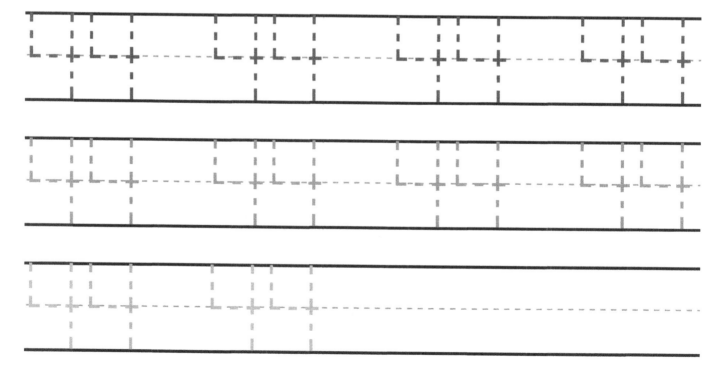

45 forty-five

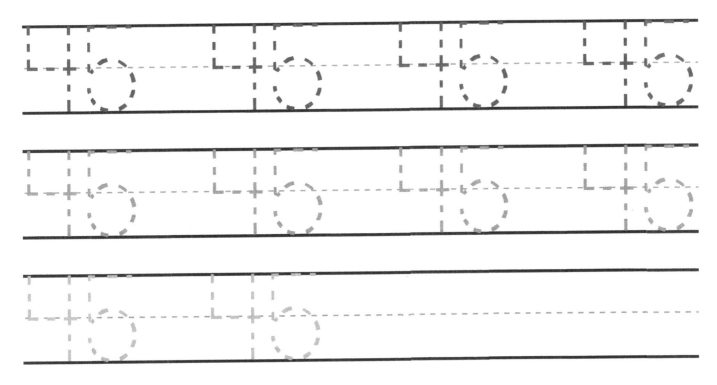

46 forty-six

47 forty-seven

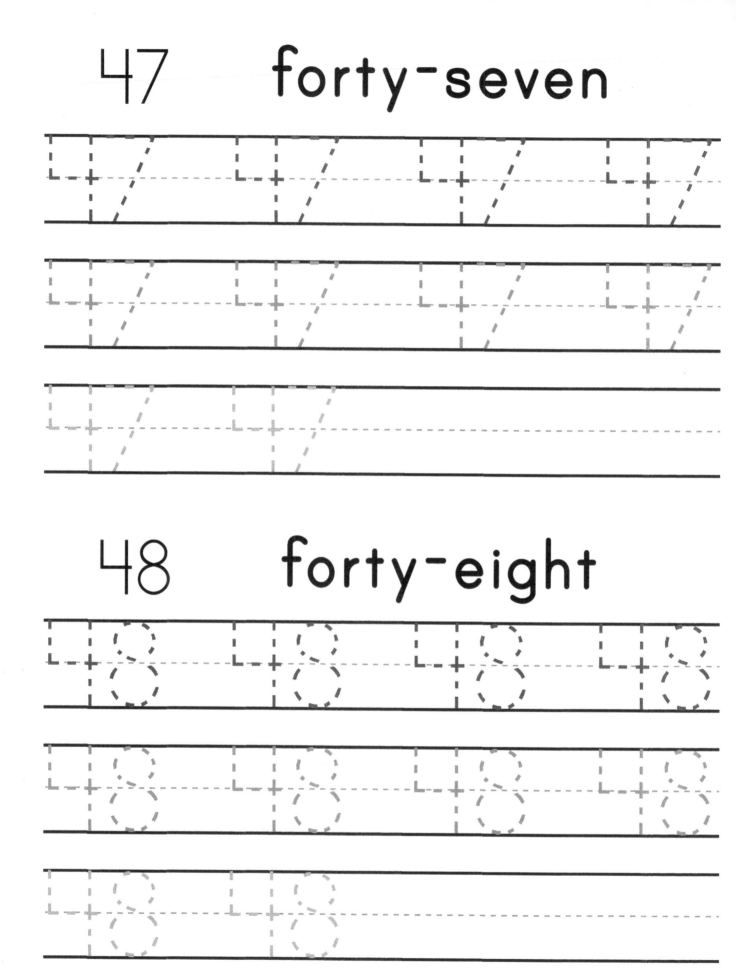

48 forty-eight

49   forty-nine

49 49 49 49

50   fifty

50 50 50 50

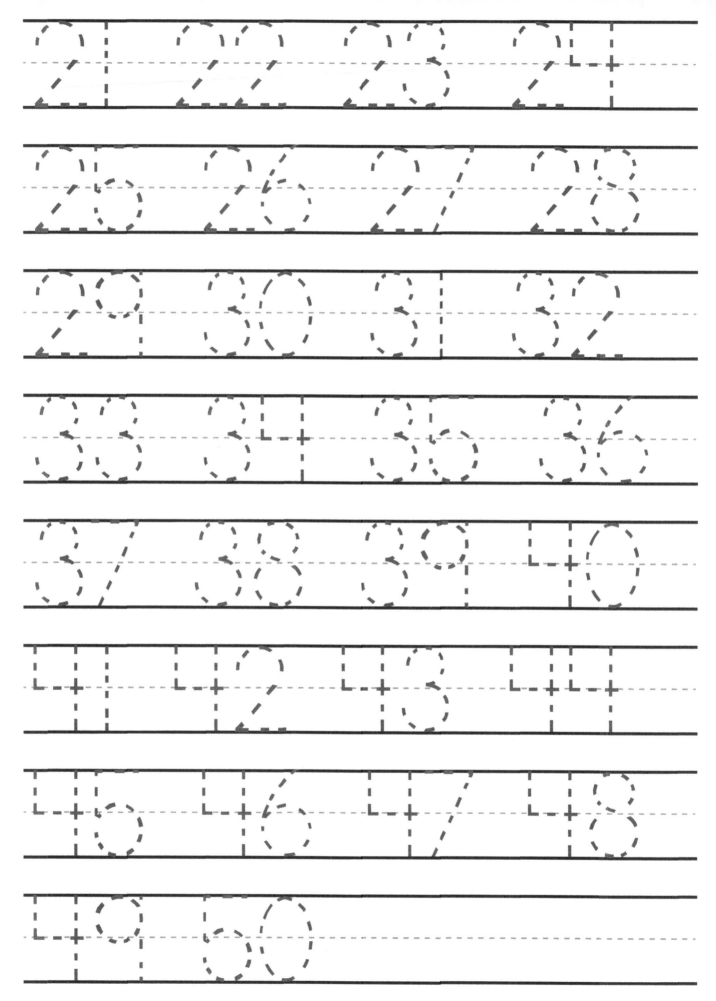

51 fifty-one

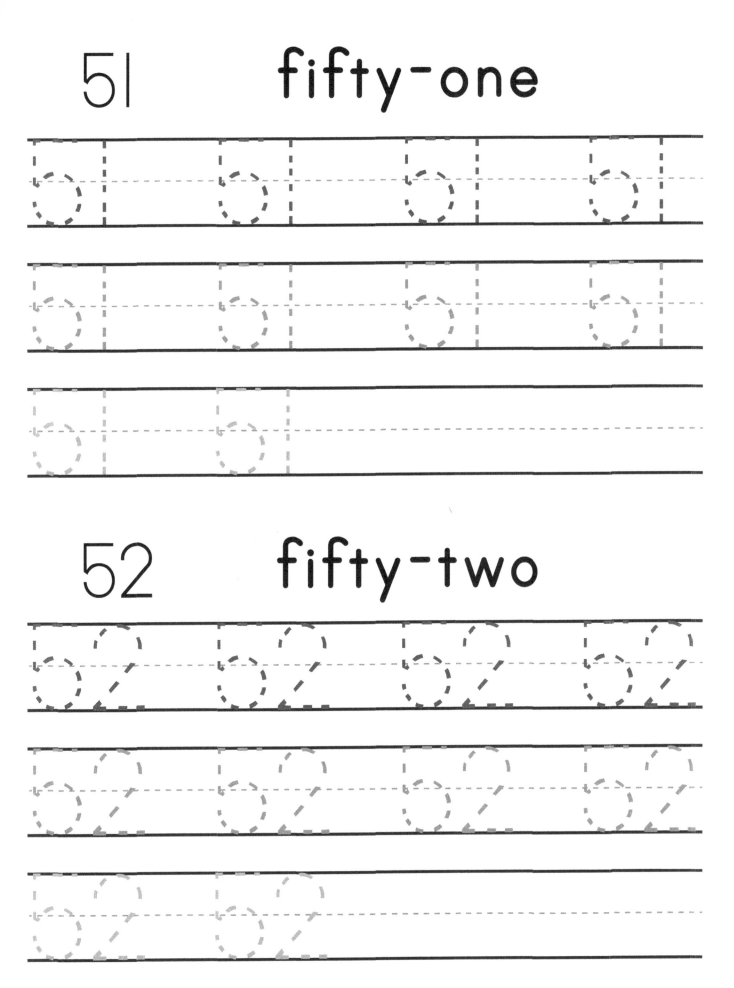

52 fifty-two

53 fifty-three

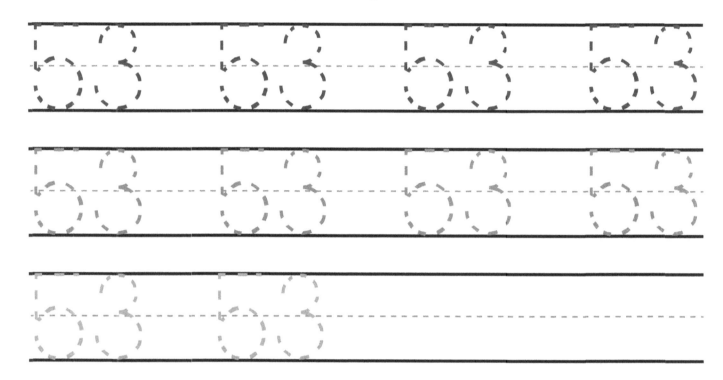

54 fifty-four

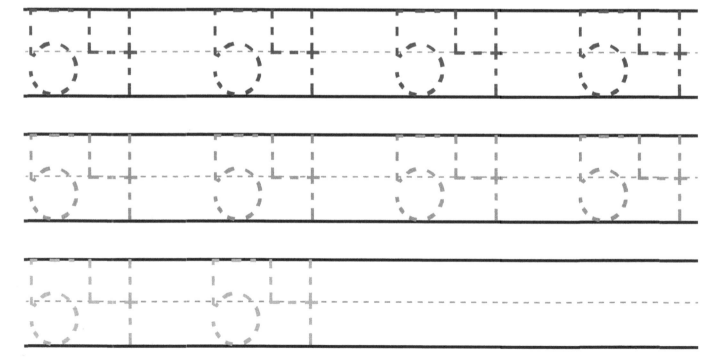

55　fifty-five

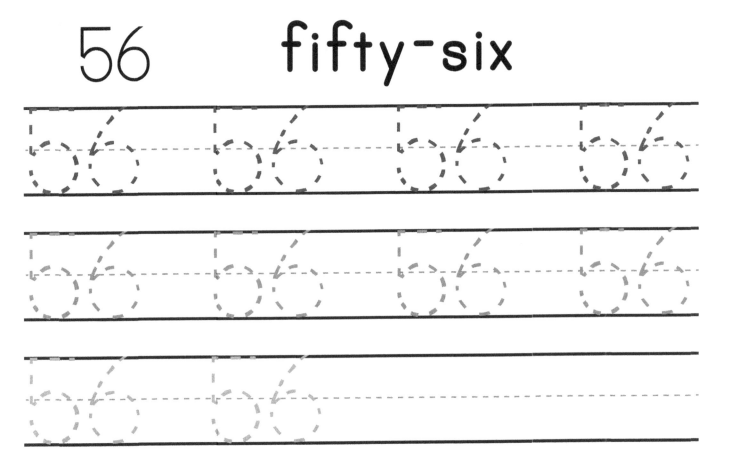

56　fifty-six

57 fifty-seven

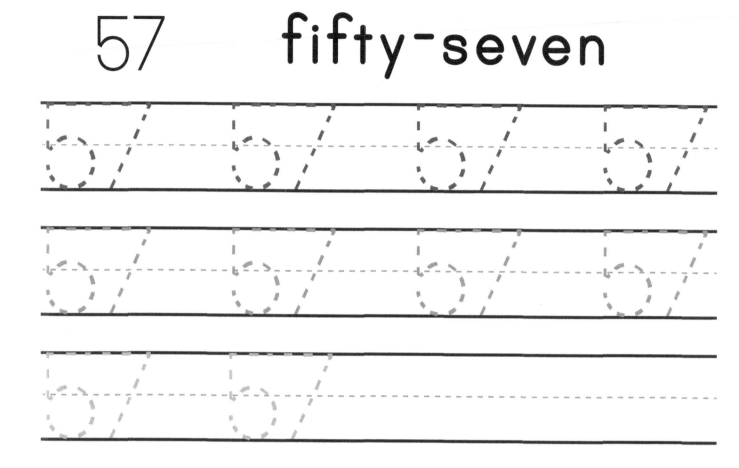

58 fifty-eight

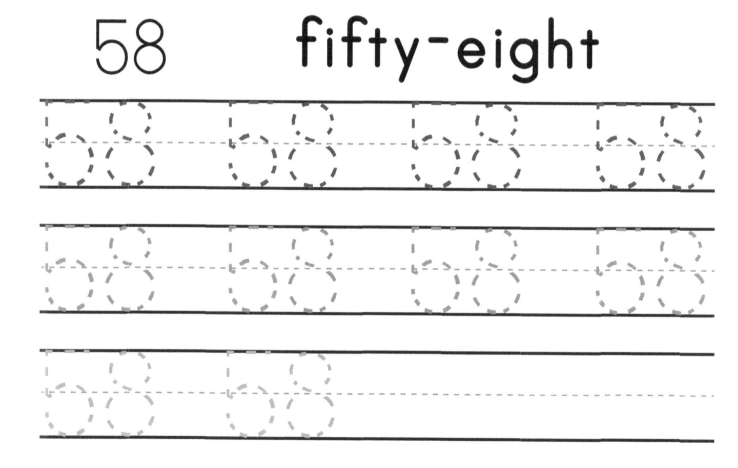

59　fifty-nine

59 59 59 59

59 59 59 59

59 59

60　sixty

60 60 60 60

60 60 60 60

60 60

61 sixty-one

6   6   6   6

6   6   6   6

6   6

62 sixty-two

62   62   62   62

62   62   62

62   62

63 sixty-three

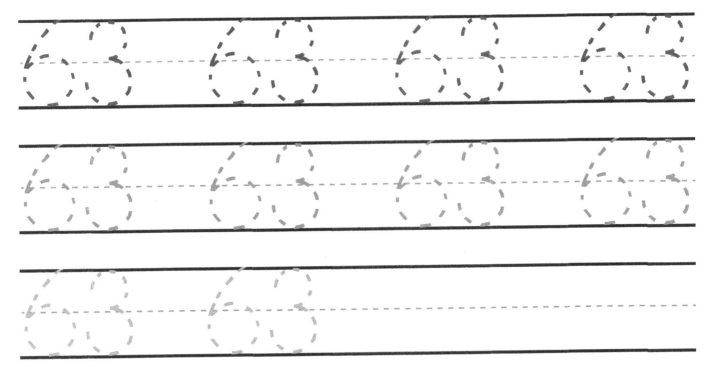

64 sixty-four

65 sixty-five

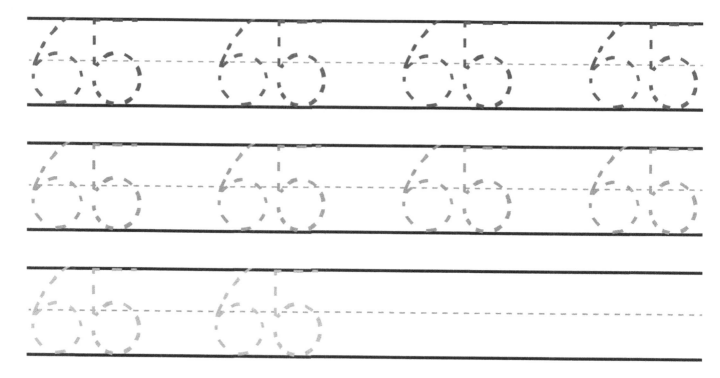

66 sixty-six

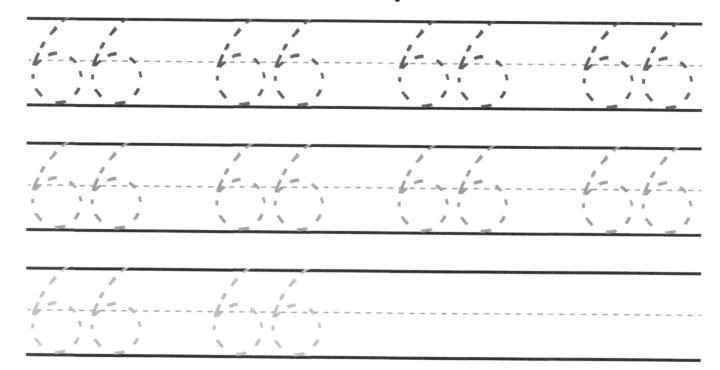

67 sixty-seven

67 67 67 67

67 67 67 67

67 67

68 sixty-eight

68 68 68 68

68 68 68 68

68 68

69 sixty-nine

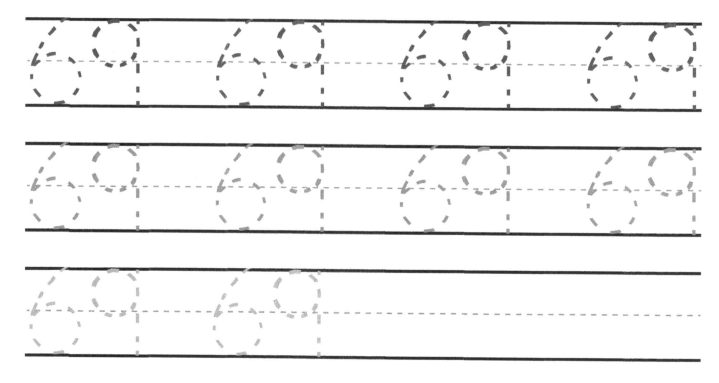

70 seventy

71 seventy-one

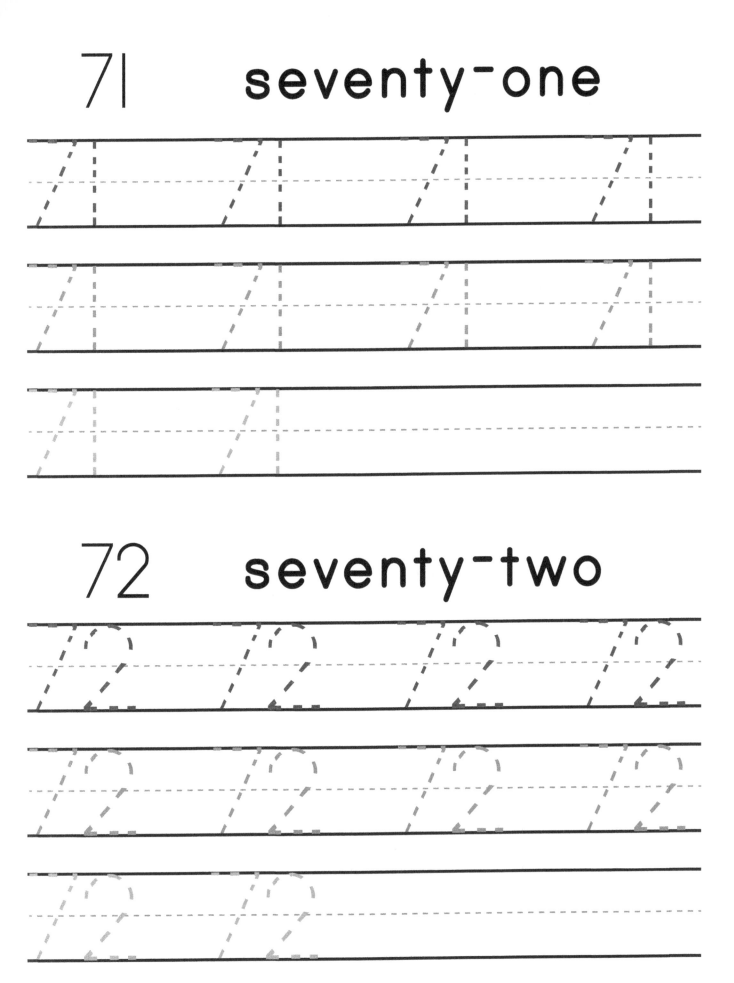

72 seventy-two

73 seventy-three

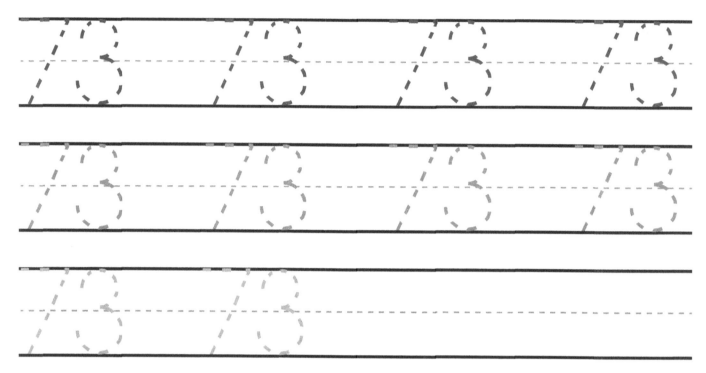

74 seventy-four

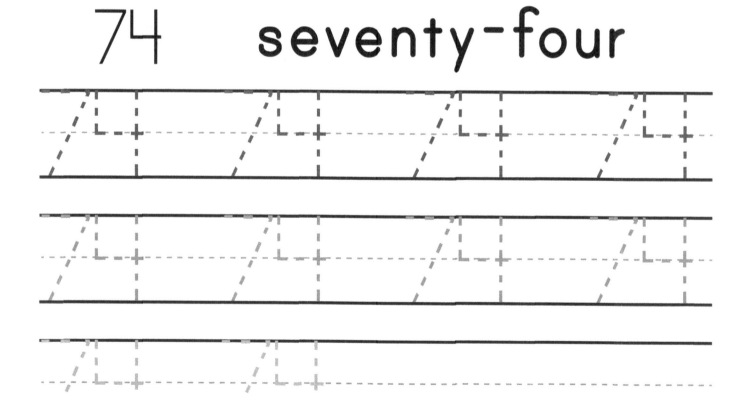

75 seventy-five

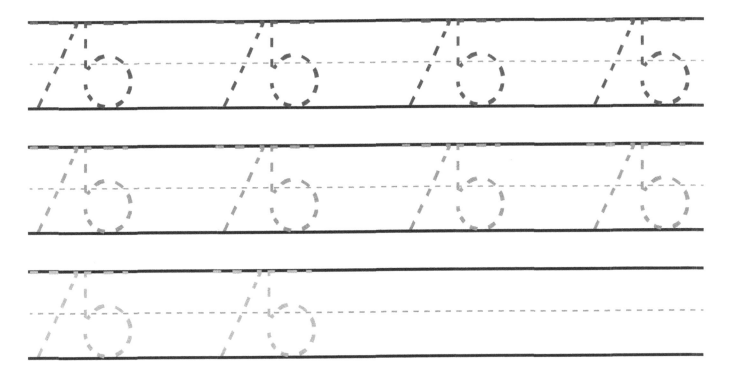

76 seventy-six

77 seventy-seven

78 seventy-eight

79 seventy-nine

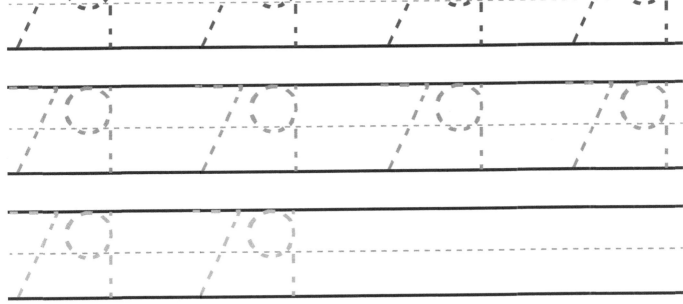

80 eighty

81 eighty-one

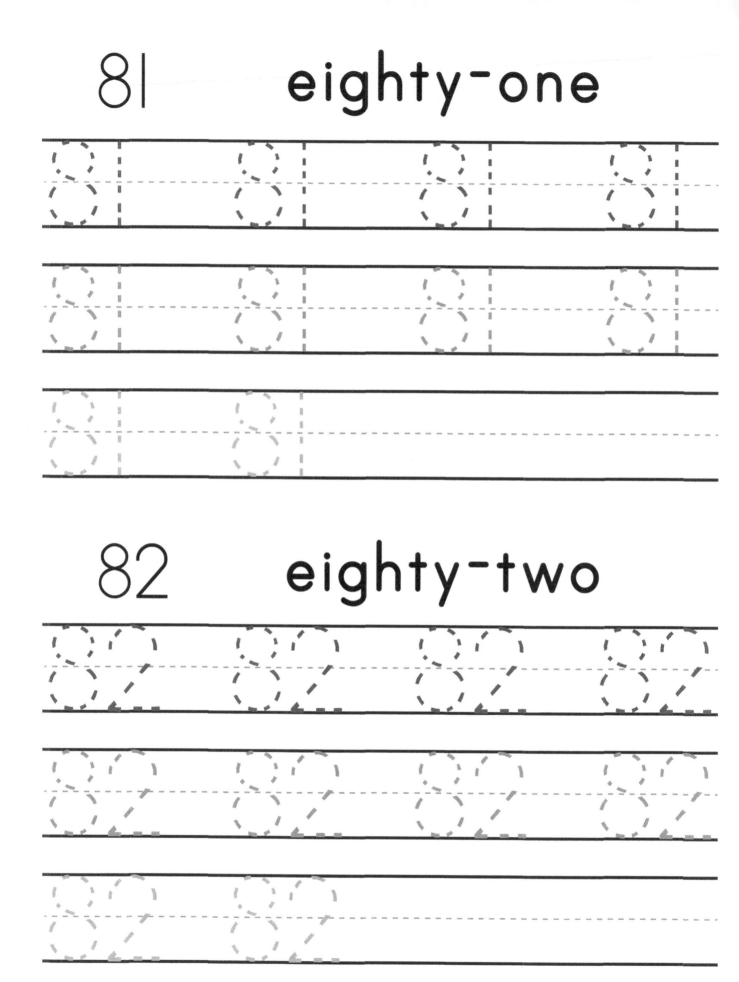

82 eighty-two

83 eighty-three

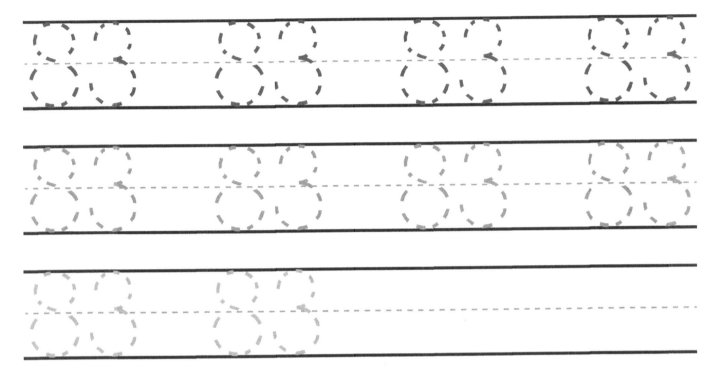

84 eighty-four

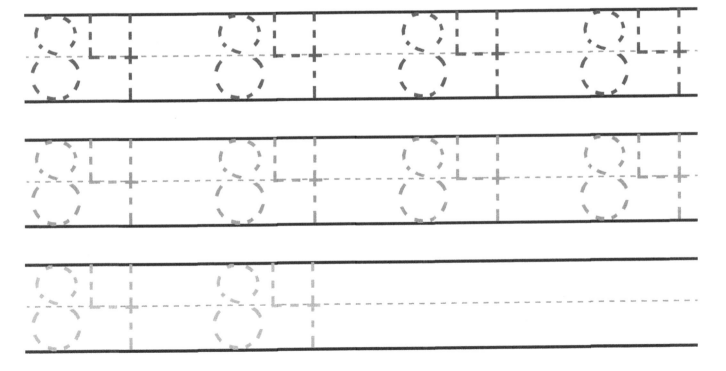

85 eighty-five

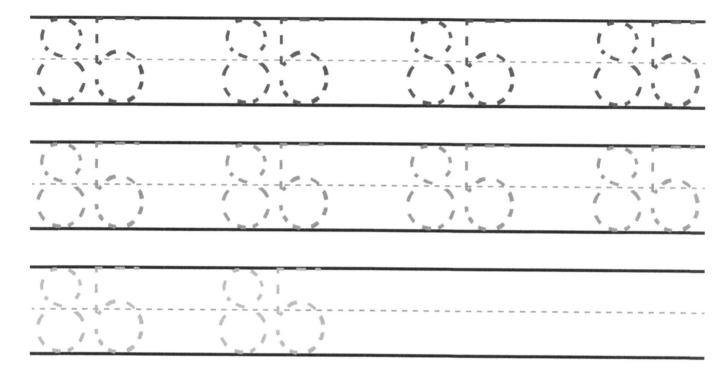

86 eighty-six

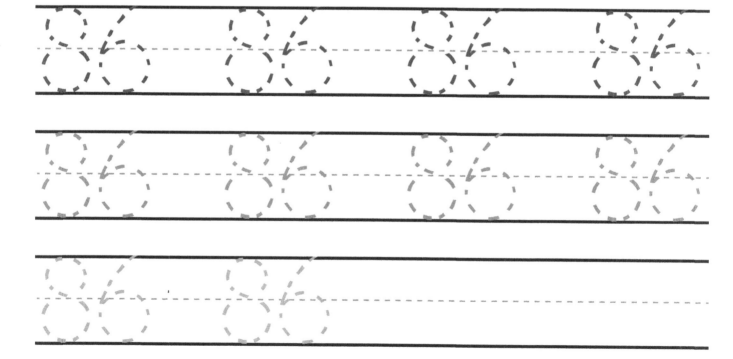

87 eighty-seven

87 87 87 87

87 87 87 87

87 87

88 eighty-eight

88 88 88 88

88 88 88 88

88 88

89 eighty-nine

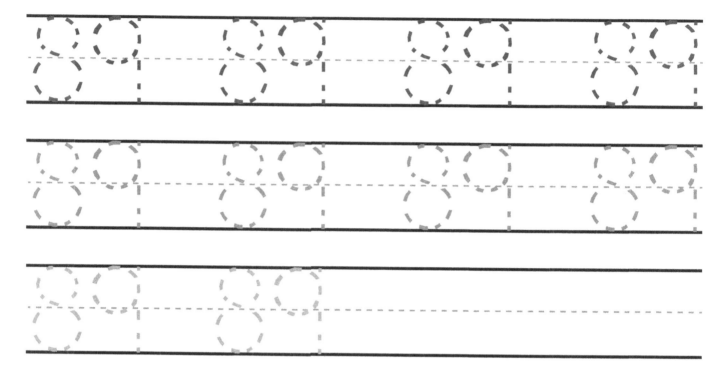

90 ninety

91 ninety-one

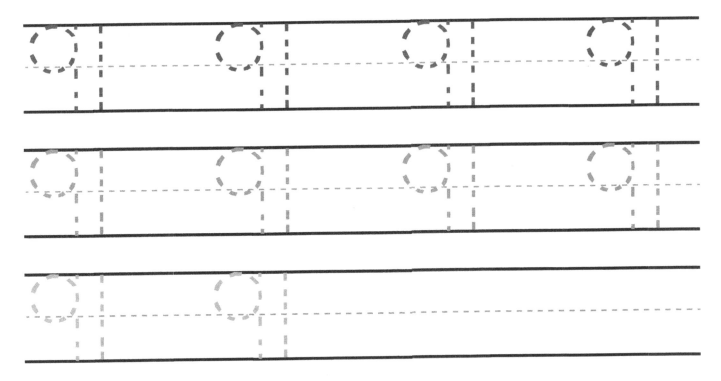

92 ninety-two

93 ninety-three

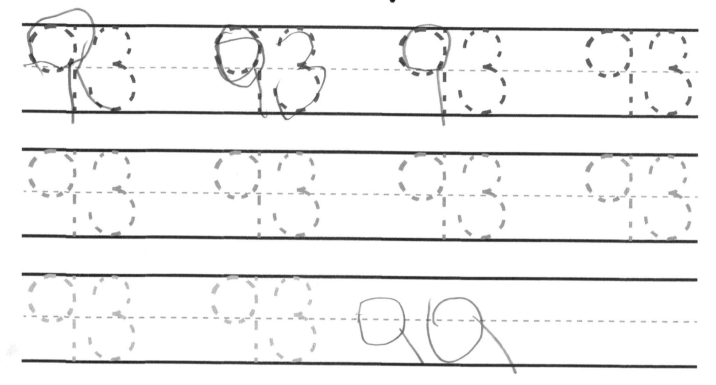

94 ninety-four

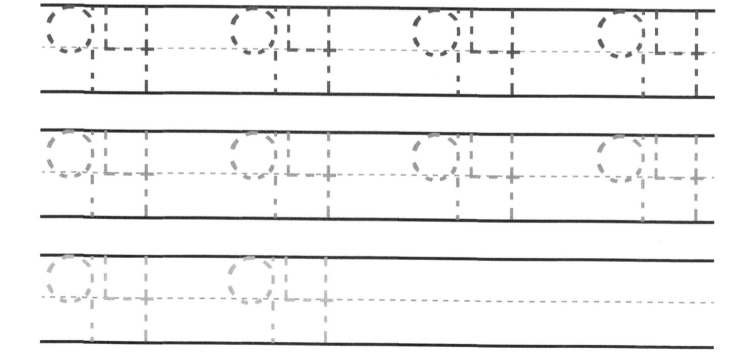

95 ninety-five

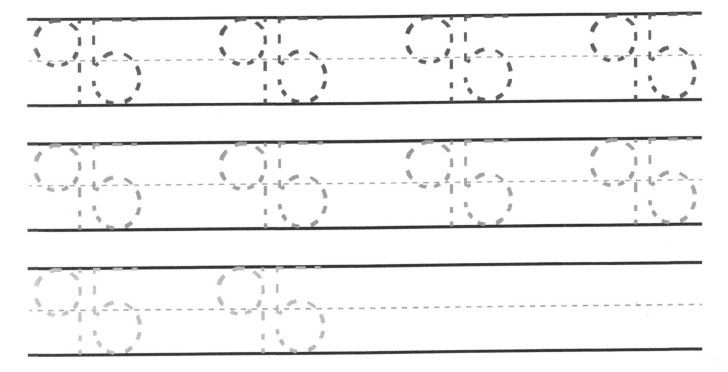

96 ninety-six

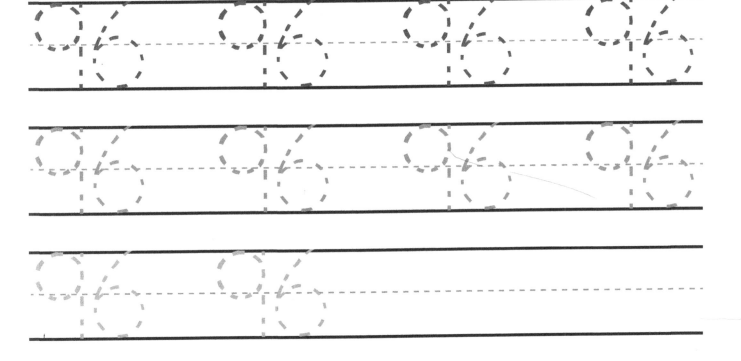

97 ninety-seven

98 ninety-eight

99 ninety-nine

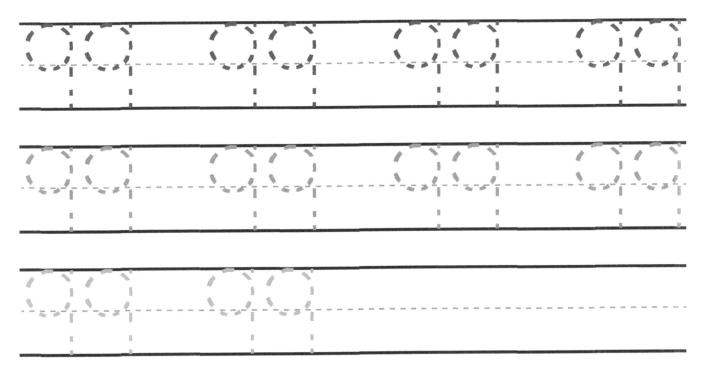

100 hundred

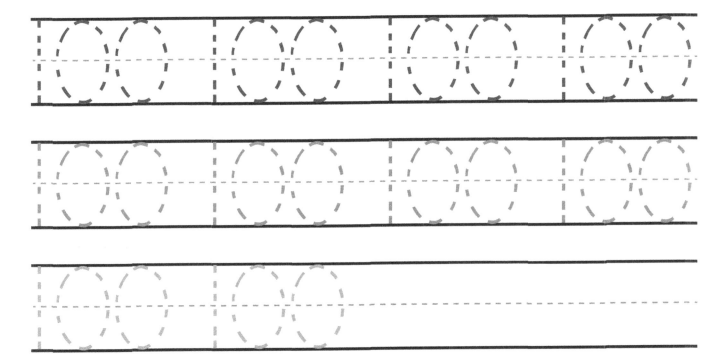

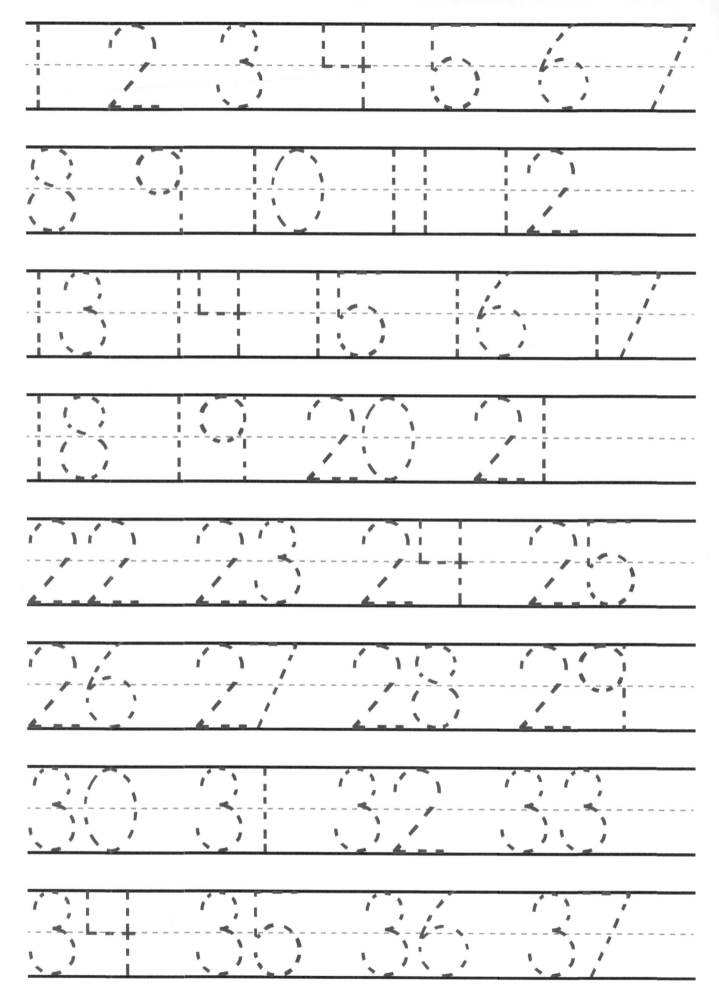

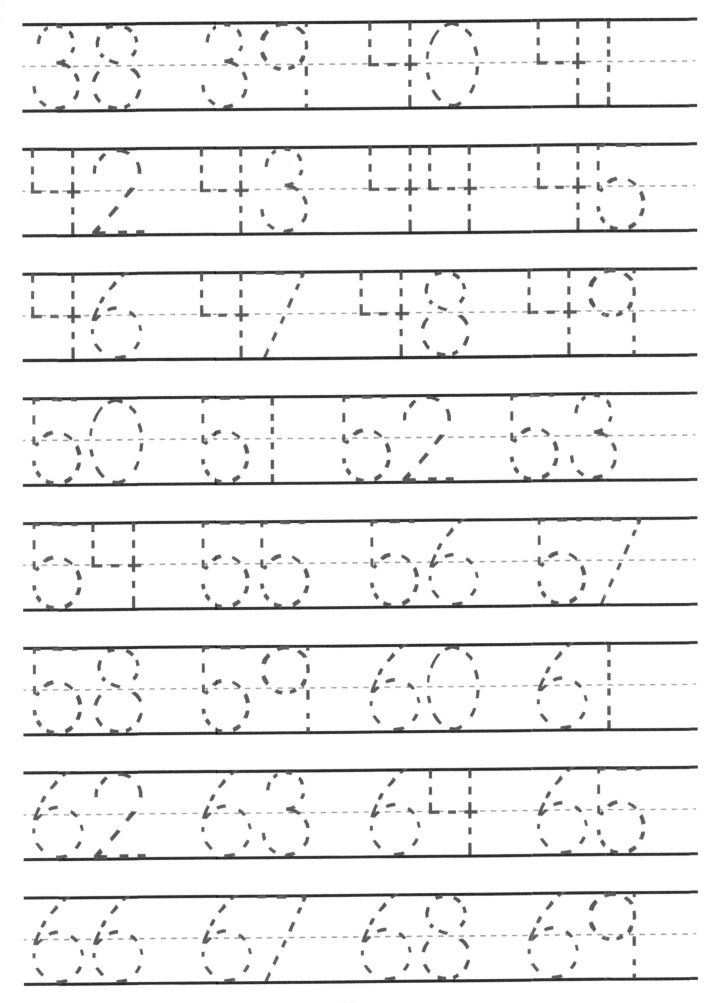

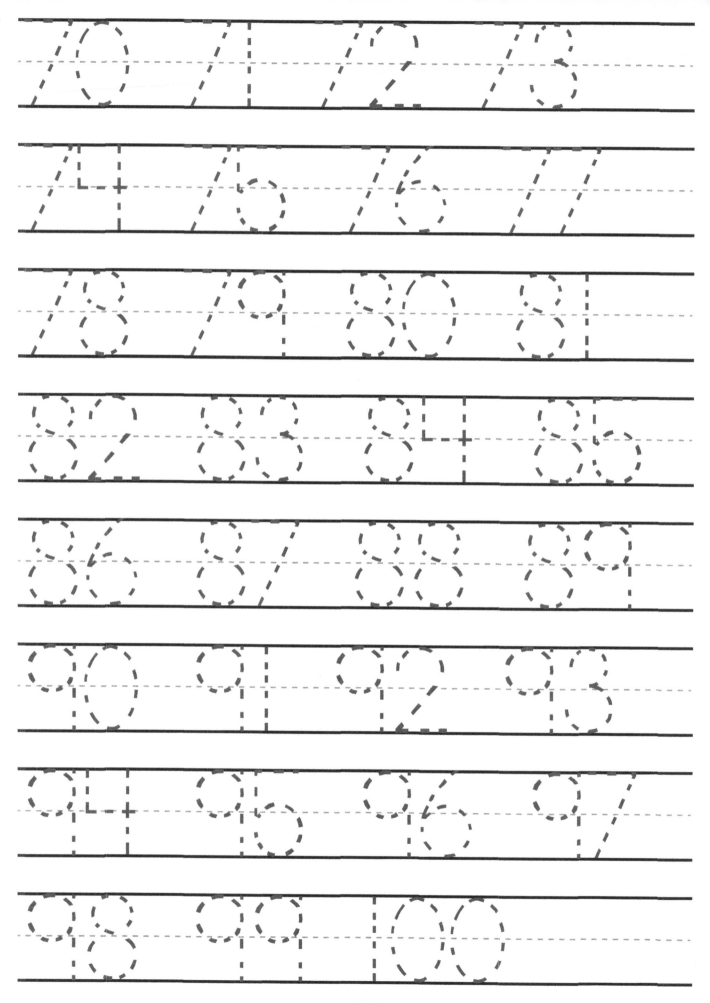

Join the numbered dots from 1 to 100 to complete the picture. Color the picture.

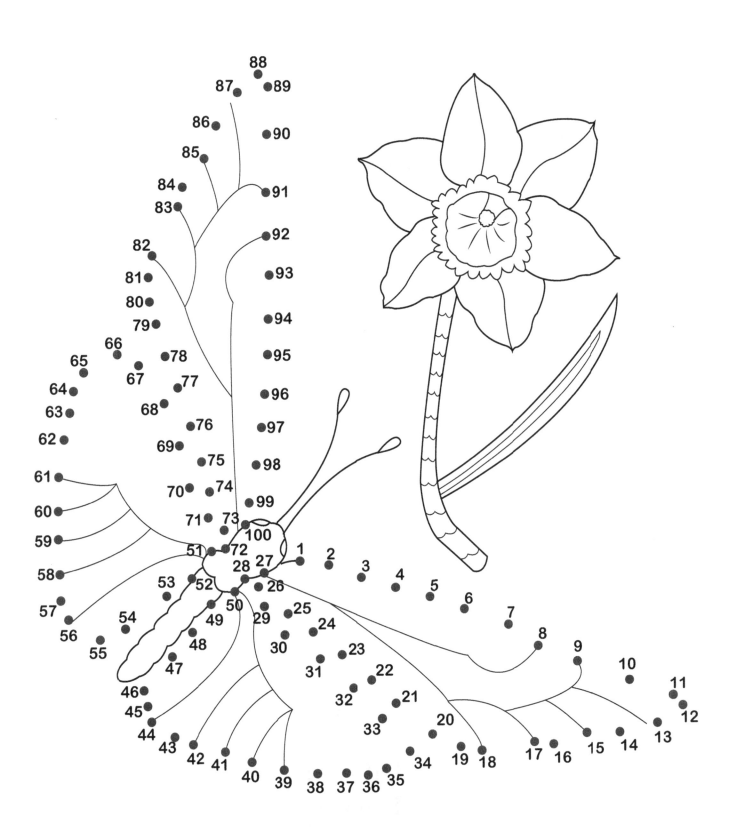

Number Tracing

Completed ✓

CONGRATULATIONS!
You are a
CHAMPION!

Recommended next skills

Hippidoo

BONUS SHEETS

Kindergarten Math
Workbook

ADDITION
SUBTRACTION

1 + 2 = 3

Number Bonds, Number Lines,
Positions, Measurement,
Skip Counting, Number Tracing

150+ PAGES

TIME & MONEY

Ages 5 - 7

Kindergarten Prep

✓COUNTING ✓TRACING ✓3D SHAPES

ISBN: 9781777421168

Math Drills

100+ Pages

Timed Tests
Addition & Subtraction
Ages 5-8

6300 Problems

Practice 100 Days of Speed Drills

✓ DAILY PRACTICE ✓ ENHANCE MATH SKILLS

ISBN: 1679103709

✓ Get it Today

Celebrate your Success!

Share the Joy!

Feel Great Everyday!

Write to me at **sujatha.lalgudi@gmail.com** with the subject:
Number Trace along with **your kid's name** to receive:

- Additional practice worksheets.
- A name tracing worksheet so your kid can practice writing their own name.
- An Award Certificate in Color to gift your child!

Congratulations
Writing Super Star
Awarded to

_____

For _____

Date _____   **Signed** _____

25

3h 25

72

43

47

71 71

7